Copyright © 2022, Larah Korrison.

All rights reserved.

Photo credit to:
Alan Shrives
Clare Croucher
Harrison Galgut
John Nutt
Larah Korrison
Nathan Williams
Oliver Bills
Paul Haigh
Shelia Huges
Simon Williams
Thomas Wilkinson
Tony Crackett
Vicky Swain

The SAGGA logo is reproduced with the permission of the SAGGA committee.

Book cover designed by Reuben Cone.

A brief history of SSAGO
Student Scout and Guide Organisation

Larah Korrison

Acknowledgements

This book wouldn't be possible without the records past members of SSAGO created and subsequently stored in their university archives. Thank you to the universities that allowed me to visit and read the materials which has helped my understanding of SSAGO's history.

I want to send my thanks to Alan Shrives for allowing me to share his superb penent and badge collection both online and through this book. The collection alone gives us so much information and insight into the organisation's past. Thank you for your time and passion.

I am grateful for the support from my close friends Georgina Westbrook and Mythili DK. I want to mention my partner Harrison Galgut for his patience and love, being by my side throughout this journey.

And finally I want to thank Reuben Cone, this book wouldn't have been as detailed without your continued effort to dig deep and keep going. I've enjoyed our calls and only slightly nervous to hear what next I needed to work on! Thank you for your invaluable input.

Contents

Chapter 1 Starting the movements	1
Memories of Jill Watkins	6
Chapter 2 Scouts and Guides on campus	11
The Duke of Edinburgh's Award	16
Chapter 3 Establishing traditions	19
Memories of Sheila Huges	24
Witan	26
Memories of Witan by Richard Harper	28
Hesley Wood / Kudu bird	32
Scout and Guide Graduate Association (SAGGA)	35
Chapter 4 The Amalgamation	39
Chapter 5 Moving with the times	45
Pennants and badges	52
Chapter 6 Parents, policies and programmes	57
Memories from John Nutt	62
Gadaffy 'Duck' Plate	64
Chapter 7 Putting the O in SSAGO	67
Cardiff meet Finnish Scouts	72
Chapter 8 Integrating the internet	75
Cutlery Cup Award	82
Mascots	83
Chapter 9 Getting back to business	87
Full membership survey	94
SSAGO Scout Active Support Unit (SASU)	98
50th Anniversary milestone	100
Chapter 10 Looking up in lockdown	105
Epilogue	114
Timeline	116
Glossary	120
About the author	122

Chapter 1
Starting the movements

To understand how the Student Scout and Guide Organisation (SSAGO) came about, we must start right at the beginning with Lord Baden-Powell establishing The Boy Scouts Association.

Lord Robert Baden-Powell was born in 1857 and as a young boy taught himself many skills that would later become immensely useful in the British Army. One of those was map-reading, which he learnt by deliberately getting himself lost in town before using the local landmarks to navigate home. He quickly saw the utility of these skills and, when he got older, went on to teach these scouting techniques to fellow men in his army regiment. In addition to being useful for the soldiers, scouting was something enjoyable and positive to focus on. Baden-Powell designed a badge for the men he taught which was worn on their uniform. It featured a fleur-de-lis, an arrowhead, that resembled a compass pointing north. Over time this badge would be approved by the War Office, and scouts were trained in all branches of the army.

During the siege of Mafeking, South Africa in 1899, Baden-Powell and his fellow soldiers trained local boys to become cadets. These boys were issued a uniform and undertook basic drills; eventually the cadets took on duties such as sending messages and keeping a lookout. Many of the cadets used bicycles to quickly move around and complete their tasks which released army men from their posts and allowed them to strengthen the front line. In recognition of their hard work and commitment, the cadets were awarded medals after the war.

In January 1900 Baden-Powell compiled notes from his experiences of training men in scouting skills and other life lessons, and published them in a guidebook. The book, called *Aids to Scouting*, was aimed at non-commissioned officers and other military personnel. However, when Baden-Powell returned from South Africa in 1902, he discovered that schools were using the book as a lesson resource and that children and the wider public were also interested in its teachings. Boys, and notably girls, were learning about observation, resourcefulness, self-care, and how to be a good citizen. Further still, young people used the skills from the book and banded themselves together to form Scout gangs. This inspired Baden-Powell to design an adapted version of the book for children. It focused on attributes useful to explorers, soldiers and sailors, professions that at the time many young boys would go on to have. It was originally created with the aim of being adapted into existing groups such as Clergymen, Country Squires, Officers of boys, Cadet Corps, Young Men's Christian Association, and sports clubs. However by 1906, Baden-

Powell had gathered enough feedback to draft a standalone version of the scheme that would become its own organisation.

In 1907, he ran a two-week, experimental camp on Brownsea Island with boys from Eton and east London. Following the success of the camp, Baden-Powell officially launched the scheme under the title The Boy Scouts Association (henceforth known as The Scouts). In January 1908, to coincide with this new movement, Baden-Powell published his next handbook *Scouting for Boys*. *Scouting for Boys* would become one of the best-selling books of all time, with an estimated 100 million copies printed in over 80 different languages.

Scout troops quickly formed all over the country; by 1909, 11,000 Scouts attended the Crystal Palace Rally, the precursor for the future National and International Scout Jamborees. Despite the fact that in this period it was uncommon for girls to hike and camp, several hundred registered Girl Scout troops also attended the first Rally. It was obvious that girls wanted to join the Scouts, therefore in 1910, Baden-Powell and his sister, Agnes Baden-Powell, introduced a parallel movement called Girl Guides (henceforth known as Girlguiding). The name was chosen from the British Indian Army regiment known as the Corps of Guides, who were known for their tracking and survival skills. Baden-Powell's wife, Olave, was also involved and became the first Chief Guide.

In 1914, Baden-Powell started to experiment with a new section of the Scouts for younger children. Wolf Cubs officially launched in 1916 along with its own handbook that provided guidance. He realised that focusing the programme on young boys resulted in good citizenship ideals being instilled early on in their life, and therefore he wanted to introduce the ideals into the movement as early as possible. However, he also noticed that older boys were just as keen to continue scouting into adulthood once they had aged out of the programme. As a result he wondered how Scouting could be extended to older boys to teach them relevant skills for the jobs they were entering. Subsequently in 1917 he introduced a new section, the Senior Scouts, which was aimed at older boys aged 15 to 18 years old. By the early 1920's this name had been changed to Rover Scouts and Baden-Powell had published a new handbook, *Rovering to Success*. The book contained detailed instructions on activities that the Rovers could organise for themselves such as service to the community and bettering one's skills and expertise. Like *Scouting for Boys*, it was also translated into many languages as other countries adopted the new section.

Baden-Powell asked a close friend, Rose Kerr to develop a programme called Senior Guides. The scheme was launched in 1918 and 2 years later the name changed to Ranger Guides. "To range" means to travel and look ahead, and this definition nicely suited the movement as this is what Olave encouraged girls to do in their community. Similarly, the term also means to "sail along a parallel line". The Ranger Guides and Rover Scouts mirror each other in many aspects. Two movements with parallel aims but different audiences, one for girls and the other for boys.

Young people were learning skills, becoming good citizens and helping their communities. These were attributes Baden-Powell sought to be important for a world where leisure time was increasing and there was a high chance for another world war to break out. Whilst the world is a different place today, those aims are still the core of both movements.

Below: Hikers at a trig point, 1970s.

Above: Manchester club weekend at Edale 1960.

Above: Manchester club freshers hike 1964.

Memories of Jill Watkins, University of Bristol, 1950s

I was one of the first inhabitants of Rodney Lodge, a newly-opened annexe of Manor Hall, and shared a large, first floor room with Mary and Pam.

In the single room next door lived Betty Mitchell, head student of Rodney and very active in the Scout and Guide Club. She was Lady President and her boyfriend, later husband, Gordon Diprose was the President – not gentleman president as this was pre-feminism and PC language. She invited the three of us in for coffee one evening and asked if any of us were Guides. I said I was so I was told very firmly that I had to join the Scout and Guide Club – no excuses – so I did. That turned out to be a decision that shaped the rest of my life.

Every year we would go on an Easter camp, food was still rationed at this time so the quartermaster had to collect everyone's emergency ration cards before they could buy any food. On one occasion, a couple of Rovers had gone into the nearest shop, some considerable distance away, to buy tinned peas for lunch. Unfortunately, when they were being strained, the lid slipped and all the peas ended up in the grease pit. No-one was very amused. We had a small meal that day. Of course, at this time, there always had to be a hedge between the male and female tents ie the camps had to be in separate fields. The idea of mixed sex tents would have caused heart attacks in the powers that be.

They say that school days are the best days of your life. Maybe, but I really enjoyed my time at Bristol University both academically and socially. Being a member of the Scout and Guide Club determined the course of the rest of my life. It not only influenced the way I did my Guiding but also led to my marriage and family with some children and grandchildren also being involved in University student Scout and Guides, and becoming Scouters and Guiders. Little could Betty Mitchell have known of the far reaching effects that invitation to coffee in October 1951 would have or of how thankful I am for it.

A note about uniform: shorts, scout shirts and neckerchiefs for the men with a miniature University badge on the back. I seem to remember they were the badges that the university cricket teams had on their caps. We wore navy skirts (any kind) with blue aertex short-sleeved shirts/blouses. There were name tapes saying "University of Bristol Scout and Guide club" which were worn on the shirts. We wore guide metal trefoil badges I think but don't remember where – we might have worn university ties. The neckers might have been black with white borders. I don't think we wore uniforms to ordinary meetings but we did when we travelled to and from camp. Most of the men also belonged to the University Rover Crew which was heavily involved in work setting up Woodhouse Park. Many University of Bristol Scouts and Guides members were scientists, doctors or vets, make of that what you will. There were Arts people but not so many.

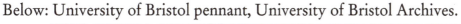

Below: University of Bristol pennant, University of Bristol Archives.

University of Manchester Scout and Guide club, summer camp 1963, hiking up Bwlch Tryfan, Wales.

Chapter 2
Scouts and Guides on campus

By the 1920s, some of the men and women who had grown up involved with the movements were going off to higher education - and they took Scouting and Guiding with them.

At the turn of the 20th century, only a select few people were able to access higher education such as university. Not only did you need to have a high level of school education, but Oxford and Cambridge universities had additional requirements. You needed to be male, unmarried, and a member of the church. Whilst there were a few colleges in the country that accepted women, generally it was uncommon for women to enter higher education. At the time, courses were limited to classical studies such as Latin, Geography, Sciences, and Maths, but as time went on, subjects expanded to attract new students. When the First World War broke out in 1914, many staff members and students from universities across the country were either conscripted or volunteered to join the war effort. Younger students who could not aid the military front would volunteer their summer vacation time by helping on the farms. In part due to this service, the relationship between the government and educational institutions improved. The government saw many benefits to universities and in the years that followed offered more financial aid for research, especially within science and technology. As a result there was a shift in focus from the established traditionally taught subjects, to those that reflected real world changes such as engineering or computer science. Whilst the Great War significantly improved technology, it also left a lasting influence on the academic landscape of the time. The rules governing who could be admitted to university changed. More women were entering higher education, with women only colleges and female professors.

The 1920s saw the introduction of university Ranger Units for female students and Rover Crews for male students. Some universities had one or the other and some had both. The first universities with either a Ranger Unit or Rover Crew were Oxford and Cambridge, both starting in around 1919. Throughout the 1920s many new crews began in Manchester, London, Sheffield, Birmingham and Bristol. Ranger Units and Rover Crews provided a social space for like minded students and ran a varied programme including camps, social meetings, hiking, folk singing, talks (such as *the craft of tent making*) and service weekends. Rover Crews in particular focused their programme on leadership training, meeting regularly and attending training courses at Gilwell, London. The Oxford club would visit local schools to show films about Scouting and held talks by various people on the Movement and how to get involved. Clubs were self-sufficient, relying on volunteers to form committees and run the programme, with many involved learning a lot about themselves and the importance of responsibility and time management.

During the early 20th century boys and girls were separated, both in education and youth activities. It was a somewhat controversial step forward for men and women to be taking part in joint activities at university. Such as joint Ranger and Rover social gatherings. The Scouts didn't allow mixed gender activities until the later half of the 20th century.

Socialising between university clubs often started with smaller events. For example, Oxford University Baden-Powell Scout Club ran a regular Halloween camp in the autumn and would invite other local clubs like Bristol and Reading. They would carve pinkies (similar to pumpkin carving), barn dance and go on day and night hikes. These interactions between clubs quickly became known as Intervarsity; the prefix *inter* means between or amongst and *varsity* relating to sporting matches. Therefore Intervarsity meant in this context activities between 2 or more higher education establishments and this term was soon used to describe all Rover crews and Ranger units at university.

Sometime during the 1920's the Oxford club decided to alter their club magazine to be a joint piece aimed at Scout clubs at all British universities. It was known as *The Boy* but what happened to it remains unclear. It stopped being produced, maybe because it became too cumbersome or perhaps the club focused more on activities for past and present members. However, Oxford and Cambridge both still run termly or annual club magazines for current and alumni members. The Oxford magazine is called *Postscript*, and the Cambridge magazine is called *Sky Blue*. They often include stories, updates, reunions and pictures. These club magazines carry valuable historical information and we are fortunate that we still have copies of them.

Many student Scouts and Guides died during both World Wars. The Second World War interrupted life with many young people joining the forces or giving up vacation tim to work in agriculture. For most university clubs it was a period of reduced activity, but for the Oxford University Scout Group as it was then known, the opposite was true. In the summers of 1942-44, Oxford ran camps at the Hill End Outdoor Education Centre for hundreds of boys whose Scout Leaders were in the forces or whose equipment had been destroyed by enemy action.

After the Second World War Scouts and Guides at universities reformed their clubs and started to patch up their inter-club activities. In order to pool their resources, many clubs merged Rover Crews and Ranger Units into a mixed gender Scout and Guide club.

Commissioned in 1941, educationists spent two years reviewing the education system in England. The *Norwood Report*, published in 1943, recommended three types of school: grammar, modern and technical. Children who did well at their 11 Plus exam tended to pick grammar schools, with a small number going to technical schools, which were also considered "selective" like grammar schools. A decade later in 1956 technical schools were given grants by the government to develop into a college of advanced technology and became a type of higher education institution. To stay on top of a developing world the UK government injected a lot of money into this new form of higher education. Courses, such as agriculture, teaching and science, were taught through a mixture of study and practical work. As a result of the increase in funding the programmes saw an increase in the number of students. There was also an increase in teacher colleges, to boost the number of science teachers available to schools. In the 1960s there was a further expansion when colleges merged together to form Polytechnics: technical colleges that focused on Science, Technology, Engineering and Maths subjects.

Just like at universities, Scouts and Guides began to form clubs attached to these colleges. The Scout and Guide clubs that were formed were small in number however the activities they did, such as camping, training and seasonal activities, were similar to university clubs. Like Intervarsity, the clubs began to work and socialise cooperatively. For example in 1954 the Leicester Domestic Science College Guide Club were guests to Loughborough's folk-song evening, where the guest speaker entertained and talked about folk singing. In 1955 the Derby Training college took part in a Christmas good turn. This was their way of giving back to their community. They raised money for 40 children in the poorer districts. The students also joined members of Loughborough on a hike through the Manifold valley and Dovedale. For them it didn't matter where in the country or at what institution students were studying in, they took part in the same activities together. The result of this was that in 1956, the Federation of Scout and Guide Clubs was formed which aimed to bring together students from polytechnics and teacher training colleges. A year later they changed the name to Intercollegiate, a mirroring of Intervarsity in goals and values.

In 30 years Scouts and Guides on campuses had formed two organisations, established themselves as hubs for socialising and developing skills, had broken boundaries with their mixed gender activities and survived a global war. By the mid 20th century clubs were established across the country at both universities and colleges, unaware they were laying the foundations for a singular unified organisation.

Below: Human pyramid at Witan 1967.

The Duke of Edinburgh's Award

One recurring theme throughout this time is the use of student input into the Movements. Whilst the focus was mainly on leadership and how to keep young people interested to stay, students also helped in pilot schemes such as the Duke of Edinburgh's award. Below is an extract from the magazine *Student Scout and Guide*, Issue 24, 24th June 1959.

"Some 600 Rangers are working for the Award through the Pilot scheme started in September 1958; of these, 300 are still at school, 25 are students and some 250 are at work. From reports received, some Guiders feel the scheme has been a great incentive to the Rangers, some think the syllabus is very similar to the Ranger programme and others that it takes too much time from Ranger work; many agreed that it was too soon to form an opinion. Many Guiders feel that some, especially those at school, will not have time to complete all the work before the final award."

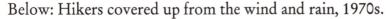

Below: Hikers covered up from the wind and rain, 1970s.

Above: Hikers at Plymouth 90's rally autumn 2017

Above: Hikers in the mist, 1970s.

Chapter 3
Establishing traditions

The post-war years was a time when student Scouts and Guides started to establish customs which would continue to the present day.

In 1947 to encourage cooperation between Scouts and Guides at both university and colleges, a magazine called *Student Scout and Guide* was published. It was sold across the UK and shared ideas, news and stories. It became the key source of information, discussion and updates and was the first of many magazines to be produced by students over the 20th and 21st century.

In *Student Scout and Guide*, Issue 13, May 1954, Clive Sutton explained to readers what he believed the aims of Rover Crews and Ranger Units were:

1. Training for leadership in the Movements. i.e. The Scouts and Girlguiding
2. Service work such as crew working weekends and practical work
3. Carrying on the spirit of Scouting and Guiding - this includes duty to God and bringing ideals into the lives of students and young people.

Frank Lowes, a Manchester and Cambridge student, developed the aims further, acknowledging the need for adaptation and change. Also from *Student Scout and Guide*, Issue 13, May 1954, he wrote:

"Who better than ourselves can free the problems that beset our own generation? Not only must we keep heritage intact, but it is our job to adapt it to our own needs, to use it fully to add something of value to it before handing it to those who follow us."

Evidently student Scout and Guide clubs were considering their aims and purpose amongst the parent movements. They wanted to be more than a social club - they sought for purpose and direction. Interestingly, the ideas developed naturally from organic self-reflection. There wasn't a formality behind the thought process; rather students met, discussed and agreed in their own time what they wanted to do and with no pressure or push from the parent movements. This theme of independence has continued throughout the history of SSAGO. SSAGO being for students and run by students is a large part of its identity - only ever being affiliated with its parent movements and never solely a part of them. As Frank mentions, the use of heritage as a way to keep on track is key to staying on the right path whether as a student, club or wider organisation.

Joint camps for student Scouts and Guides are called rallies. The first rally was a week-long summer camp run by Birmingham at Beaudesert, Staffordshire in 1947. Rally goers would visit local university towns and cities, go on hikes, hold a formal dinner, run campfires and barn dances. Rallies occasionally included some campsite service as well as a conference, an opportunity to discuss topical subjects in the Movements and updates on upcoming events. Noteworthy, the following two rallies were run by The Scouts (1948 at Clitheroeand and 1949 at Youlbury), before it was then handed back to university students. Every year rallies were organised by a different club in their area, and largely focused on a theme, such as Religion or Youth in industry. Due to the different education programmes and a strict capacity for the camps, Intercollegiate students were not invited.

At the rallies there were regular meetings between the National Executive committee and a representative from each attending club. The National Executive were, and, still are elected students who take on the leadership of the organisation. The meetings were called the SSAGO Full Committee but became known as Reps. The purpose of the meeting was to discuss matters affecting student Scouts and Guides. Such as leadership training, travel to rallies, organising rallies and information from the parent organisations. At the meeting the reps would share updates about their club including what activities they've done recently, what they have coming up and any other highlights. These were then scribed into the minutes. As technology came into society the organisation changed the process with reps submitting their reports ahead of the meeting. They were then available to read alongside the minutes which saved time and allowed for longer discussions at Reps. The reports have provided an important archive of how typical clubs were run over the decades. By reading old minutes members revel in how little has changed in the organisation, how clubs run the same activities year in year out and how the same conversations come up time and again. The original materials also create a vault of ideas for clubs to be inspired by and can help members track how active their club has been in the past.

On the 3rd January 1958 at Guide Headquarters, London, 25 Intercollegiate representatives attended the Student Scout and Guide conference for training colleges. At the meeting speakers from The Scouts and Girlguiding recognised how influential their Movements were to the transformation of Scouting and Guiding in education institutions over the last fifty years.

The conference also opened the floor to discuss how Rover Crews and Ranger Units should operate at colleges. The attendees came up with:

- Individual clubs would be open to all students regardless if they have been a Scout or Guide
- Clubs would help the local community, including links to troops and companies. But students do not have to volunteer if they do not want to.
- Clubs would operate regionally, with cooperation between local universities and colleges such as joint meetings
- On a national level, there would be a week-long training camp at the end of August, with support from previous Student Scout and Guide members who had been to rallies.

The structure is largely the same today with clubs helping their communities, individuals from all backgrounds being welcome to join and the strong cooperation between clubs across the country. This conference laid the foundations for the direction that Intervarsity and Intercollegiate would go on to take.

At a club level, some universities and colleges formed specific Scout and Guide clubs, whilst maintaining a separate Ranger Unit and/or Rover Crew. The programme for Scout and Guide clubs were more focused on social activities and speakers whilst the crews and units continued to focus on leadership training and serving the community. Scout and Guide clubs ran parallel to Rover Crews and Ranger Units. Students could choose the type of programme they wanted to follow; for example if they wanted to focus on their leadership skills they would join the Rover crew or Ranger unit.

At the end of the 1950s the Student Scout and Guide magazine was given a refreshed look, including a new name and design. Kudu was published briefly and continued to engage with Student Scout and Guides across the UK. Its name came from the South African Antelope called a Kudu from which Baden-Powell used the horn, by blowing into it to wake up the Scouts on Brownsea Island.

By the 1950s, Rovers and Rangers at higher education institutions had found ways to share knowledge and keep in contact. Many traditions that were started during this time are still felt today, a testament to how similar students can be regardless of how much time has passed. Having a common interest and desire to work together helped shape the Intervarsity and Intercollegiate organisations. Students were willing to give up their time and contribute to the magazines, national camps and club meetings. It wasn't long before the two organisations decided to become one.

Below: Halloween, dancing in the barn at Hill End, Oxford in 1968.

Memories of Sheila Huges, University of Bristol, 1950s

I signed up to the Scout and Guide club at the Fresher's Fair in the Victoria Rooms in September 1951. I knew one already, Peggy Neath and she had been an assistant warden at the harvest camp in 1950 attended by a group of girls from Commonweal School, Swindon. We had continued to correspond, and it was good to meet again. It meant an immediate social group in the new college world. Contact with the group was through a dedicated noticeboard in the union rooms and early events included an evening campfire and Sunday hike.

In 1953 I went to the Oxford Club's Halloween weekend and danced on Eynsham bridge at midnight after a party including traditions as bobbing for apples in a tin bath. Invitations were often sent to other S&G clubs where members elsewhere could be accommodated. Alan Hazell and I went by train to Swindon, my father met us and drove us to Witham Woods, leaving us rather worriedly as it was dark and wet. One Easter meeting was to the cinema to see "The Ascent of Everest" Gill Fisher and I shared our 21st birthday at Manor Hall. We each were given a signed book by those attending, all from the club! Each name brings back memories and Gill and I still correspond and occasionally meet.

Below: Group photo Youlbury 1955.

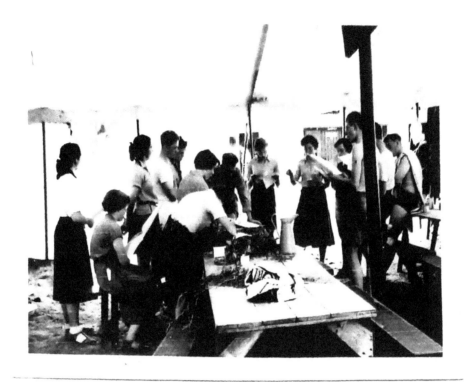

Above: Choir practice at Youlbury 1955.

Above: Campers at rally 1955.

Witan

The UK wasn't the only country in the world to have Student Scout and Guide clubs. Many other countries set up their own such as Australia, Norway, Austria and Canada. After the devastation from the Second World War, Student Scout and Guides wanted to rebuild links across the world.

In 1959 at Gilwell Park, London the Oxford club hosted the very first international camp for student Scouts and Guides. It was called Witan, named after the Anglo Saxon term Witenagemot meaning "meeting of the wise".

Until the 1990s, Witan was a regular camp hosted by a different country every two years and continued to be an opportunity to make friends and share experiences.

By 2000 Witan had stopped, likely due to the complexity of running the camp and losing links with International student Scout and Guide groups. There was an attempt to revive Witan in 2007 but this fell through.

In 2012 a new style Witan camp was held at the Kandersteg International Scout Centre in Switzerland. This Witan had no international attendees and focused more on adventure and exploration. The camp was successful, if a bit complicated to organise. Another new style Witan was held 4 years later in Berlin, Germany where attendees took part in expeditions, visiting the local area and water sports. The international element of the camp wasn't achieved largely because links with clubs abroad had fizzled out of existence.

Right: First Witan at Gilwell, London. The Scouter June 1960.

Above: Attendees at the 1986 Witan.

Above: Witan 1988 Dorset, England shirt design.

Memories of Witan by Richard Harper, University of Oxford, 1963-1965

In Norway, at least, some students organised a club and hosted a Witan in 1963. I was one of a party from Oxford who travelled by minibus. The camp was held on a lake called Lyseren. This was a proper Scout camp with patrol sites where we cooked our meals. My main memory of the camp is that we had one beautiful day of sunshine but for the rest of the time it was overcast or raining. Apart from campfires there was simple Norwegian country dancing, also out of doors, and it was not easy keeping on your feet on a sloping and increasingly muddy field.

Typical of Norwegian Scout camps is the overnight hike. Map reading was no problem because we simply walked round the lake. As there was forest most of the way, the idea was that we would not take tents but make a bivouac. Given the inclement weather, some patrols cheated and went round on the first day but we had taken the precaution of taking with us a large plastic tablecloth that was part of the patrol equipment and with that placed among branches cut from trees, we kept dry. I remember one English girl saying, "My mother would have kittens if she saw me now." Whether this was on account of the bivouac or the fact that she was sleeping in mixed company, I do not know.

In 1965 the Witan was held outside Hamburg. This was a rather different affair with food served indoors. I always remember some cheese that made the dining room smell like a toilet just after someone has used it, although it tasted much better than it smelled. I found myself, on the basis of my O Level German, trying to give a summary of a lecture by a German professor about European history. I knew he kept going on about the Congress of Vienna, but I could only guess at most of what he had said. After the camp, I was one of those who took up the offer of a trip to Berlin. It was not so long since the Wall had been built and the authorities obviously wanted people from abroad to see how things were, so the trip must have been heavily subsidized. It was a memorable experience!

Below: Witan 1963 pennant, both sides.

Above: Cambridge club at Witan 1967 dressed up in their formal attire for the international day.

Above: Flag break at Witan 1967.

30

Below: Witan 1959 pennants.

Hesley Wood / Kudu bird

At the 1956 annual conference, Intervarsity was presented with 10 guineas and a small antelope horn carved into a bird. The kudu had been shot by Sir Harold West near the river Nile. Sir Harold West, was a prominent Scouter in the Staffordshire area, notable for the acquisition of Hesley Wood campsite.

The Manchester club was tasked with providing a box to house the antelope horn, which was eventually completed in 1960. The horn and box were presented as *Hesley Wood* and by 2000 it was more colloquially called the *Kudu bird*. The carved antelope horn would sit on the left-hand side of the National chairman at meetings. Then for a period during the early 2000s it was passed from rally to rally and contained rally mementos.

In 2017 the Kudu bird was taken out of circulation because the original box had become full of items putting pressure on the delicate wings of the bird. A year later SSAGO paid for a conservator to clean the box and repair its broken wing. It's now taken out for special occasions for everyone to admire.

Below: Kudu bird box, presented by Manchester in the 1960s.

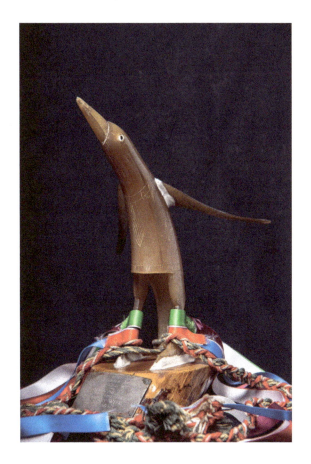

Above: Kudu bird. Plate engraving reads, *Presented by Sir Harold West to the Intervarsity Scout and Guide Rally Hesley Wood 1956.*

Scout and Guide Graduate Association (SAGGA)

During the late 1950s ex-students were attending rallies as a way to reunite with their friends and stay in contact with their club. Shelia Reed wrote in *Student Scout and Guide, Issue 16*, 1956, "*Very few of one's contemporaries are left and a new generation of students are there. Yet no one wants to stop coming - to forget the rallies and everyone one knew there*". At the time an informal group of ex-students would meet in London and they called themselves the *Peter Pan Club* - because they never grew up. There was an acknowledgement that whilst students became graduates, they did not stop being Scouts or Guides. Many people were involved in other organisations that held reunions and would stay in touch and something similar was proposed for Intervarsity and Intercollegiate.

In 1957 the Scout and Guide Graduate Association (SAGGA) was formed. Its aims were, and still are, to provide service to the community and young people whilst also being a way for graduates to stay connected. It operates through groups spread out across the country, typically based on geographical regions. SAGGA is one of The Scouts and Girlguiding support groups, offering service to campsites and events. One example includes Tandamania, which launched in 1979 and involved 188 teams of Scout and Guide patrols being challenged to prepare a meal for two people including table decorations, gifts and entertainment. From a social perspective, SAGGA regularly holds a summer camp, where they take part in crew work at a campsite and go offsite to visit local attractions. They run skiing trips to places like Kandersteg, Switzerland as well as SAGGA's Alternative Rally, their version of a SSAGO rally, designed to be a soft introduction for new members who may have just left SSAGO.

If The Scouts and Girlguiding are SSAGO's parent organisations then SAGGA is it's older sibling. In 1978, SAGGA held a seminar at Aston University called *Democracy and Power in the Scout and Guide Movements*. Student Scouts and Guides were invited to the event to listen and take part in the discussions. SAGGA has always offered support to students at universities, by providing guidance and impartial advice. SAGGA members, many of whom were once SSAGO members themselves, have a better understanding of how SSAGO and its members work than The Scouts or Girlguiding. In the present day, most returning officers for SSAGO's annual general meeting are SAGGA members as many once had the experience of running in these elections themselves in the past.

Below: SAGA trip to Norway 1965 badge, image by Graham. Note the use of SAGA before it became SAGGA

Above: SAGGA 1961 camp attendees

Above: SAGGA 1965 pennant.

Above: SAGGA mascots. Named SAG and GA.

Above: SAGGA members at SSAGO Reunion 2017.

Above: SAGGA membership badges

Chapter 4
The Amalgamation

At a time of review and updating, members were considering a unified organisation that could give student Scouts and Guides an improved experience. This move would solidify the organisations in the changing Scouting and Guiding landscape.

During the 1960s both The Scouts and Girlguiding reviewed their programmes and uniforms with the aim to modernise and appeal to a new generation. Societal changes meant the youth were taking greater interest in equality and diversity, and these beliefs rippled into youth programmes.

In 1967, The Scouts published the *Chief Scout's Advance Party* report. From the findings, the Senior Scouts and Rover Scout sections were replaced with Venture Scouts for 16 to 20-year-olds. Similarly, in 1966 Girlguiding published their report *Tomorrow's Guide* which also saw a change in uniform style, programme and training standards. Members of Intervarsity, Intercollegiate and SAGGA were called upon to contribute to the report by taking part in feedback sessions and attending talks. The Scouting and Guiding programmes moved away from preparing young people for war and shifted their focus on teaching modern relevant life skills, with the programmes being continually revised ever since.

In 1957 two Redland College, Bristol students applied to go to the Intervarsity Summer Rally at Foxlease, Hampshire. Their disclosure of being students from a training college led to heated discussions about the principle of accepting Intercollegiate members into Intervarsity summer camps. By this point summer rallies were topping the one hundred mark, which at the time was seen as max capacity. Therefore there were concerns over whether opening the doors to non-university students would affect Intervarsity's ability to run rallies. In the following years members wrote passionate pieces in *Student Scout and Guide*, putting up a wall of hard words which led to misunderstandings. Discussions were brought up again in early 1960 when only sixty people attended the Summer Rally - likely because more young people were travelling abroad during their summer vacation. Similarly, although the Intercollegiate rallies had been firmly established, there were only about thirty people in attendance, so neither organisations were reaching the extraordinary totals people were expecting.

To build relationships on the ground, universities and colleges began experimenting with cooperation between clubs. This meant joint activities, sharing knowledge and helping each other. What they realised was that university students and college students were not so different to one another. Some clubs even discovered college students amongst their membership, masquerading as one of their own because they too wanted to be part of a social group. Nevertheless the idea that Intervarsity and Intercollegiate should merge to form one unified movement was still too bold of a step for many. However in 1964, the *Robbins Report* investigated changing the higher education system substantially by proposing to grant charter to Polytechnics, therefore allowing them to issue degrees. The change in higher education structure would affect the Intervarsity and Intercollegiate relationship, putting students from both movements on equal grounds. Given their mirroring values, goals and format it became apparent how mutually beneficial it would be to join forces.

In 1966 serious discussions on merging started to take place. Amalgamating the two organisations would carry benefits and risks. A unified student organisation would have a greater overview of the landscape across higher education institutions and better control over its finances but may be too complex to run with greater numbers - would rally capacity reach its limit? These were risks that the membership were largely willing to take however, and in February 1967 the *Student Scout and Guide Organisation* was officially formed. At the Spring Rally AGM the membership voted on the name, the options were:

- The Educational Scout and Guide Organisation
- The Student Scout and Guide Organisation
- Inter College-Varsity Organisation
- National Scout and Guide Club Committee/Conference
- Inter Rallya

We now know which they chose and it was probably the best option! The organisation was granted permission to use the SAGGA emblem and continues to use it to this day; it's a combination of the Scout and Guide emblems with unique green and yellow colours. There is still some feeling that SSAGO should design its own emblem, rather than borrow an already established design. However, both organisations using the emblem does help unify SSAGO and SAGGA as related organisations. The formation of SSAGO didn't affect the membership - in fact they hardly noticed any changes. The records available aren't clear whether there were elected people to run Intervarsity and Intercollegiate. Nor do the

41

records state what format the running of the predecessor organisations looked like. However, we do know that from 1967 SSAGO formed the National Executive committee, a team of elected officers they were: Chairperson, Secretary and Treasurer. The formation of SSAGO allowed the National Executive committee greater influence over the finances. And it paved way for all students to come together regardless of their institution of study.

For many years The Scouts and Girlguiding had a representative for their organisation's presence at universities and colleges. The representative for Girlguiding explained their opinion of their role in *Kudu Notes, Issue 3*, October 1969: *"Someone to be on the touchline at SSAGO discussions, to get the feeling of the atmosphere and trend of thought among the thinking future leaders of Scout and Guide Movements."* The parent organisations acknowledged the role that SSAGO played in the larger arena of student Scout and Guides. It was no secret that for many years both parent organisations struggled to keep young people interested as they reached adulthood, especially those that went to university. SSAGO has always played a big role linking students with local groups and maintaining a space for leaders to be with peers that share similar values and opinions.

In *Kudu Notes, Issue 10*, October 1969, the Girlguiding Headquarters adviser for Guiding in universities and colleges said that SSAGO was necessary but so were the Headquarter representatives from The Scouts and Girlguiding. Throughout the rest of the 20st century there was a strong relationship between the parent organisations and SSAGO. There was always a dedicated staff member who would go to SSAGO AGMs and National Executive committee handover meetings, usually the same person every year. The parent organisations were able to understand what mattered most to young people and utilised SSAGO in some programme changes that came about from trying to modernise their Movements. The representative role responsibilities changed alongside The Scouts and Girlguiding restructuring and redundancies and by 2000 the role ceased to exist leading to a difficult relationship with SSAGO. Many following National Executive committees have had to reintroduce SSAGO to The Scouts and Girlguiding, an exhausting process but necessary to stay relevant in the forever changing landscape.

Merging the two similar organisations was a controversial topic during the 1960s. Those in

42

favour of the change saw how the benefits outweigh the risks. However, it wasn't always easy to present this to passionate club representatives. With hindsight and a lot of history, today we can see that this was a good decision. The late 1960s was the right time to amalgamate: the changes to higher education meant that there was less elitism between university and college students. Streamlining themselves into one organisation led to a unified approach to branding, purpose and values. This was the first step in becoming a modern and relevant organisation for students at both university and polytechnics. Around the same time a Spring, Summer and Autumn rally became a fixture in the student Scout and Guide calendar and this remains to this day.

Mike Day from *Kudu*, Issue 31, Autumn 1962

"If you have ever been to an Inter-varsity summer conference you might be excused for thinking like me that there could not be anything else like it. Surly nowhere else can you find three-quarters of those present apparently not understanding a word of what is going on and the remaining twenty five percent either trying to depose the chairman or to make some trivial amendment to an even more trivial motion as though their lives depended upon it. Well, if you thought that, you are wrong. I discovered this summer that the inter-varsity conference is not unique. The inter-collegiate one is exactly the same."

Below: Patrol at the Summer Rally in 1967 organised by Birmingham in Packington Park.

Chapter 5
Moving with the times

During the 1970s The Scouts and Girlguiding reviewed their uniforms, badges and programmes to suit the modern world. Like the parent organisations, a new generation of SSAGO members swept through and brought with them changes to the way rallies were run. There is a constant need to stay relevant or face redundancy. But these changes were not without controversy.

By 1969, just two years after amalgamating, members of the newly formed SSAGO questioned the lack of achievement from the organisation. At the time the constitution stated that SSAGO should 'be a forum for discussion about matters that affect Scouts and Guides'. Yet in *Kudu Notes*, Issue 2, March 1969 students from Leicester pointed out that these discussions could only happen at rallies and so far organisers hadn't included time for this in their programmes. This was not a conscious decision however, but an example of the shift in attitudes during the 1960s. Students moving through Scouting and Guiding were different people to those that joined in the previous decade and with this came a change to rally programmes - away from discussion and more towards fun and adventure. As mentioned before, Scout and Guide clubs were social in nature, compared to Rover Crews and Ranger Units which were service led and focused on advanced leadership training. The 1960s were a crucial period of social change and at the same time many established Rover Crews and Ranger Units merged to form one Scout and Guide club. Young people were paving the way to a new world that was fair for all and societal norms were being challenged alongside the previous generations' expectations of SSAGO. Members of SSAGO wanted to go away for the weekend to see friends, meet new people and have fun exploring the local area. Thus there was less interest in formal discussions and spending most of the weekend talking. SSAGO phased out these old traditions that were seen to be no longer relevant to the membership - a pattern of adaptation we constantly see from the organisation.

The 1970s was a pivotal moment in deciding SSAGO's direction. Not only did SSAGO amalgamate from Intervarsity and Intercollegiate just 3 years prior but the new organisation was very different in its outlook. A new generation of young people were joining higher education with a fresh perspective, but some older members felt that SSAGO was drifting away from its roots, particularly at rallies. In *Kudu Notes*, Issue 6, October 1970, Richard Billinghurst, 1970 Chairman, asked members to think about whether SSAGO should be taking a more intellectual approach to Scouting and Guiding and what it was that members should be doing at rallies. By this time, rally was still a place for student Scouts and Guides to meet, share ideas and serve the community but now it was doing so in a different, more contemporary way. For some members the change was difficult to witness; Richard said "SSAGO is becoming too social in its outlook and there's no room for discussions".

The Scouts and Girlguiding have always called themselves Movements. This is because they move with the times, they adapt and change to remain appropriate for young people. In a world that was constantly changing, SSAGO would have to learn to do the same. As a result, Richard explained in *Kudu Notes,* Issue 6, October 1970 that at Cambridge Spring Rally of 1971 there would be a patrol based system so that members can get to know each other. He said, "There will also be no usual Saturday afternoon activities, as these have now degenerated into a holiday activity; SSAGO is not a travel agency!". This particular edition of Kudu Notes exemplifies this big change in SSAGO's history as the membership was split with differing views. From the same magazine John Barker offers his thoughts on the matter, "I go to rallies to enjoy myself and see more of the country. Not to spend it all day cooped up inside." This mixed approach to the schedule made the Cambridge rally a success. The programme included spending Saturday morning touring Cambridge followed by a talk and debate about leadership and responsibility in the afternoon. They held the usual evening activities - the barn dancing and campfire remained - and on Sunday morning they held a Scouts and Guides Own and the annual SSAGO conference (or AGM as it is called today). Those that went said that there was never a dull moment at the rally and that they enjoyed the mixture of fun activities with the more intellectual ones. They noted that the speakers were interesting to listen to, which likely helped fuel debate and engagement.

At the Leeds Summer Rally in 1970 the Reps decided to turn the week-long summer camp into a weekend because between 1968 and 1970 rally attendance had been low. There was a constant difficulty to find members and clubs willing to run the camps, so by shortening the event it would be easier for them to organise. This is the time when SSAGO firmly established its triannual rally programme and from this point onwards a club or group of members organised a weekend rally in the autumn, spring and summer. However some summer rallies still offer members an extension to their bookings for extra days at the campsite, allowing them to make the most of their travel and time.

By the summer of 1975 *Kudu Notes* was discontinued and was replaced with a termly publication produced by the Chairman and Secretary called *SSAGO Newsletter.* The aim was to send out information at a higher frequency so that everyone was aware of the changes as they occurred. At the same time *Bulletin* was published, primarily written by the Secretary and was a page or two long with brief updates and information for committees and members. The use of published magazines continued into the late 20th century as a form of communication within the community. Clubs would cascade messages by word of mouth and sharing information from the magazines. However word-of-mouth has always been the best method of promoting clubs at universities. In 1975 the Bangor club shared its experiences of making links with local Scouting and Guiding communities. The club held a static stall at the regional Scouters conference. It was an opportunity to let leaders know about the club, what activities they did and what SSAGO did across the UK. The club said it was a successful event and helped to boost its links and awareness.

By the end of the 1970s SSAGO had brought itself into the modern world and had adapted to a new generation of students. To stay relevant it had to change and move with the times. Rally numbers climbed back up and membership grew with new clubs opening across the UK. It had finally found its footing and was beginning to draw more attention from its parent organisations.

Below: Pennent from the 1967 Autumn rally hosted by Loughborough Scout and Guide club.

Above: Manchester club weekend at Edale 1960.

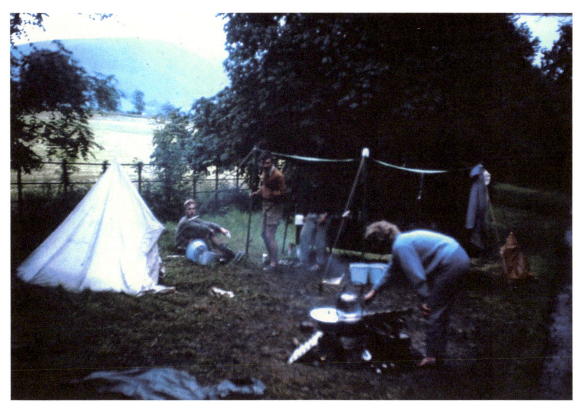

Above: Patrol preparing food at summer Rally 1963.

49

Rally in Bangor 1968.
Photography was an expensive hobby so there are not as many photos of student Scouts and Guides compared to today.

Pennants and badges

Badges have always been a core part of Scout and Guide movements. To earn a badge gives a sense of achievement and success. Membership badges were introduced to give unique identity to groups including those at university. Part of the registration process with The Scouts headquarters was to agree on a membership badge design. The designs were heavily influenced by the university crest and imagery and they help identify when university Rover Crews and Ranger Units were registered.

Over time Rally pennants were issued at the National Events. Their design included the theme, location and/or club hosting the event. Fortunately this means there is now a solid record of the dates, themes and locations of past events.

In the late 20th century, pennants made way for an expansion into other merchandise in the form of membership badges, pin badges, t-shirts, stickers and ties. The supplies from sales are put back into the running of SSAGO such as, paying maintenance fees and buying even more merchandise.

Below left: 40th Anniversary badge
Below right: SSAGO badge

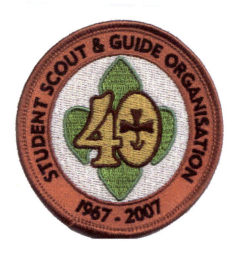

Above left: Swansea club badge
Above right: University of Bristol International cooking competition badge 2001

Above: Imperial college Rover Crew pennant

In 1963 Jenny Millest submitted a design for SAGGA to use. It was approved at the AGM of the same year. The green represents The Scouts (before they changed to purple) and the yellow represents Girlguiding. The emblem has taken on other colour combinations such as red and white.

When SSAGO was formed it was given permission to use the SAGGA emblem. It was formally registered with Scout HQ in 1980. A pin badge version was approved by Girlguiding HQ around 1984. Since then it has been an iconic image for Student Scout and Guides in the UK. The design has largely remained the same and clubs incorporate it into their merchandise.

Above: Registration date of the SSAGO badge dated 12/11/1980.

Above: SSAGO blanket badge.

54

 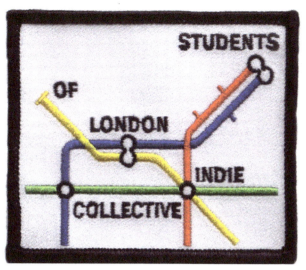

Above left: Federations of Student Scouts and Guides badge.
Above left: Students of London Indie Collective badge. For students studying at any London university.

Above left: Sheffield University Scout and Guide club badge.
Above right: University of Bristol Rover club badge.

Chapter 6
Parents, policies and programmes

SSAGO demonstrated to the parent organisations that when young people reached adulthood they were keen to continue their Scouting and Guiding experiences. SSAGO's format provided the balance between adventure and community service.

As SSAGO evolved The Scouts and Girlguiding had a vested interest in its development. The magazines that SSAGO produced were circulated to The Scouts' and Girlguiding's relationship secretaries so that they were aware of what the organisation was getting up to and the views it shared. Each year the publicity secretary for SSAGO would encourage clubs to send articles in for the newsletter, whether that was a report on club activities, views and ideas or club programme suggestions.

In *Secretary's Notes*, Issue 2, 1979-1980, Russell Barry the SSAGO Chairperson, encouraged members to consider how clubs could improve relations with the parent associations. The approach was open to interpretation: does SSAGO wait for the parent organisations to approach them for advice or does SSAGO independently review The Scouts and Girlguiding then inform them of their views and suggestions? Who's role was it to review how SSAGO and The Scouts would work together and to what extent SSAGO would be governed - a topic that frequently comes up over the decades. For example, in the aforementioned *Secretary's Notes*, SSAGO at the time was described in The Scouts' *Policy Organisation and Rules* as followed:

I 85iii
The Student Scout and Guide Organisation exists to: provide a forum for discussion about matters that affect all student Scout and Guide Clubs and their members and to act as a channel of communication between the Headquarters of the Scout and Guide Associations and the student Scout and Guide Clubs.

I 8 iva
A student Scout and Guide club exists to… utilise the special training of its members in critical appraisal and discussion of all aspects of the Movement and, by research, to develop a sensitivity to new ideas in the field of youth work and the presentation of suggestions to help towards improving the quality and effectiveness of the Movement.

Also in *Secretary's Notes*, Issue 2, 1979-1980, Tony Allen the relationship secretary for The Scouts, praised SSAGO for its efforts in continuing what it stood for. Saying *"…the fellowship offered by each club to students is of vital importance in preserving the image of*

Scouting as an up-to-date youth organisation". He encouraged clubs to do more service work with local Scouting districts as a way to give back to the community and supported more young people continuing Scouting as they grow up. Likewise, Anital Manusell, the publicity secretary for Girlguiding acknowledged the value of meeting the SSAGO National Executive committee face to face. Anita goes on to mention, *"You all have the opportunity to prove to your contemporaries that Guiding/Scouting has relevance today and faces the problems and attitudes of society without the exclusiveness and complacency which are so often attributed to the two associations"*. It is clear from these comments that at the start of the 1980s the relationship between SSAGO and it's parent organisations was strong.

However just four years later The Scouts produced a report, *Scouting in Education,* which looked into whether Scouting could be introduced into schools as part of an extra-curriculum programme. The report suggested closing SSAGO and using the structure of clubs at further education institutes such as colleges and sixth forms. Predictably this potential threat to closing down SSAGO had to be addressed immediately. SSAGO considered itself a necessary body whose functions could not be carried out alone by The Scouts. The suggestion was never realised; SSAGO continually demonstrated that students can run a national organisation and could adapt itself organically. Unlike The Scouts and Girlguiding, due to the constant flow of new members bringing new ideas, SSAGO has never had to introduce large formal reviews. As the membership changes so does the direction of the organisation. The *Scouting in Education* report also looked at SAGGA, the outcome of which meant that, much to its members disapproval, SAGGA was unaffiliated from the movements. It is evident that The Scouts and Girlguiding had much influence on SSAGO and SAGGA. Both organisations had to demonstrate their value or face being unaffiliated and always kept one eye on it's occasionally overbearing parents.

Later on in the decade The Scouts set up a working group to review SSAGO. The group's findings were published in 1987. They noted the following:

1. SSAGO should be encouraged to elect officers (National Executive committee) to SSAGO who have the time and commitment to carry out the work of the organisation and to ensure that, where possible, there is some continuity provided by electing at least one of the officers of the outgoing committee

2. Outgoing and incoming National Executive committee members meet with The Scouts and Girlguiding representatives as soon possible after election and induction.

3. The annual conference agrees on a work plan for the upcoming year.

4. Each Association appoints a member of staff with the responsibility of maintaining relationships and working with SSAGO.

5. Each Association does more to promote SSAGO and continues to support the work of SSAGO, including the production of materials to promote clubs.

On the whole SSAGO has continued to function with the above recommendations in place. National Executive committee members are voted based off their manifesto points then at the handover agree the plan for the year ahead. During this time the relationship with The Scouts and Girlguiding continued to be strong with annual meetings during the handover period and strong communication throughout the year. The parent organisations did promote SSAGO for many years after the report was issued. However, in the 21st century the parent organisations haven't been able to appoint a staff member who's role is to maintain relationships with SSAGO. As a result SSAGO has had to promote itself to The Scouts and Girlguding members, with many people not knowing about the organisation until they get to university.

During the 1980s Girlguiding were trying to keep the 18+ sections relevant. Girlguiding introduced *Link*, a section for aged 18 to 30 year olds, mainly for members who could not commit a lot of time to a unit. During the 1990s however, The Scouts were losing 30,000 members a year, so in 1995 it set up another Programme Review which would launch The Scouts into the new millennium. From the review Venture Scouts were replaced by two new sections: Explorer Scouts (14-17) was launched in 2002 and the Scout Network (18-25) was launched in 2001. Whilst SSAGO was not part of the Programme Review, the organisation was encouraged to get in contact with their local Network County Commissioner. The Scouts highlighted that it did not intend to take over SSAGO and valued the unique link it provided to The Scouts and Girlguiding. SSAGO was keen to get involved, such as learning from Scout Network and providing some insight and guidance. As an organisation with knowledge on students and that particular age range you would expect The Scouts to leap at the chance, unfortunately, despite efforts to contact staff involved in Scout Network there was no response. SSAGO's ever evolving nature exemplified how 18+ members wanted to conduct themselves in the Scouting and Guiding communities. Meanwhile The Scouts would continuously review Network as it attempted to keep the programme relevant to today's youth but the section has never achieved the same level of engagement as SSAGO. With hindsight there was a missed opportunity not have SSAGO involved in the organisation of the aged 18 and above sections.

During this time the parent movements were going through internal restructuring. Unfortunately for SSAGO this meant investigating who their main contact would be. Until the mid 1990s SSAGO has held a strong relationship with its parent movements in the form of relationship secretaries. After many years of struggling to find a new contact, the impact is realised in the early 2000s when SSAGO has to explain what it is and how it functions to the new representatives. By the time this relationship is understood a new National Executive committee is elected and so is a new staff member given the role of meeting SSAGO. Both start again every year causing difficulties in continuation and moving beyond the getting to know you stage. It must have been frustrating for National Executive committees to go through this process.

SSAGO has always maintained a close relationship with The Scouts and Girlguiding, it follows their rules and regulations and takes advice on processes and procedures. SSAGO is a unique organisation for young adults, not many can boast its ability to be self governing and run solely by volunteers who are mostly under the age of 25. SSAGO has and always will be an opportunity for students to take leadership roles, to work with peers and grow a strong community of passionate Scouts and Guides.

Above left: SSAGO, Scout and Guide badges
Above right: SSAGO club badges and necker banner

Memories from John Nutt, University of Birmingham, 1963 - 1968

Fifty years ago there were far fewer universities and the numbers of students were smaller so Scout and Guide clubs tended to come and go a little over time. There was however an established pattern of a termly rally and the Intervarsity organisation had as its main function the maintenance of a contact list of the various clubs and the arranging of which clubs would organise the future rallies. This usually involved a little persuading or arm twisting but in my experience was not too difficult. Clubs were usually aware that taking on this role could be quite onerous for the people involved.

At this time rallies in the autumn and spring were usually held in a school with use of the kitchen for catering, classrooms for sleeping and the hall for the usual Saturday evening Ceilidh.

Numbers were around 250 so the dancing was crowded and often very well received by the band and caller as there was no struggle to get people on to the floor and a good proportion knew the dances. It was here that I first came across 'Ninepins'. This is a version of the Cumberland Square dance with an extra person in the middle whose purpose is to swap with one of the others while avoiding getting hit in the charges across.

Below left: Pennant from the Invervarsity Rally hosted by University of Birmingham Scout and Guide club 1963.
Below right: University of Birmingham Rover Crew badge unknown date. Club founded in 1929.

Above: Birmingham Scout and Guide club annual photo from 1965.

Above: The group that went to Norway in the summer of 1968.

Gadaffy 'Duck' Plate

In 1984, SSAGO attended Witan in Florence hosted by the Italian university clubs. During the weekend, the Libyan Scouts brought with them commemorative plates and gave one to each of the visiting countries. It is not known what happened to the plates given to those outside the UK, but the Bath club on their drive home decided to turn theirs into a competition. They wrote out the rules and presented it at the Autumn rally. Since then, the plate has travelled across the UK, and clubs have fought to win the prestigious prize.

Competitions slowed down during the 1980s onwards, and it would not be till 2017 that the National Executive committee restarted challenges. In 2007 the Aberdeen club designed and gifted SSAGO a box to keep the plate in. In 2018 the quartermaster updated the box into a flight case to better protect the plate and book. The box is now used by SSAGO's archivist to store paper records and artefacts.

Summer 1985 competition Bath vs. Liverpool: 7 a-side tug of war
Summer 2018 competition Cambridge vs. National Exec: Punt Joust

Below: Gadaffy Duck Plate (left) and log book (right)

Above left: Gadaffy 'Duck' Challenge plate box made in 2007.
Above right: Member holding the Gadaffy Duck Plate and book in the flight case.

Above: Recipients of the plate at the 1984 Witan. Image from log book

Chapter 7
Integrating the internet

Technological advances during the 1990s gave SSAGO an opportunity to put itself firmly on the map. It changed the way it could communicate and share ideas and started to give National Executive members time to focus on other duties.

During the early 1980s, the *SSAGO Journal* took over *Bulletin* and *Secretary's Note* as SSAGO's main publication. It followed the same format as its predecessors; it was mostly published on a termly basis, containing member submitted articles and relied on sales to maintain publication. However during the late 1980s and early 1990s, the internet had started to integrate into universities and SSAGO could utilise this new piece of technology.

Notably the 1989 autumn edition of *SSAGO Journal* includes the first mention of electronic mail, or email as we know it to be. Obviously, compared to the usual snail mail method, this was faster and more convenient. The editor encouraged members to share rally information through email and from here SSAGO started its gradual transition away from paper to an electronic system and email.

During the late 1990s SSAGO set out more notable changes. Firstly at the 1996 summer Reps meeting it was agreed to use the new website to publish minutes rather than posting them out to clubs. The website provided SSAGO the opportunity to send information out quickly and more frequently than ever before - a process that eventually became even faster with social media. The website gave SSAGO the tools to organise itself, provided club committees with resources such as forms and it was a place to talk via forums to other club members. It was also a central landing area for prospective members.

SSAGO Journal lasted until the mid 1990s, when students could increasingly access computers and the internet. Then *SSAGO News* was introduced as the first SSAGO magazine produced on a computer. The use of Microsoft Word allowed the Publicity Officer to create visually appealing publications which could be edited before distribution as either emails or printed copies. Around the same time SSAGO's first website was created and it was used to share information about the upcoming national events. Organising these events was easier too as the internet allowed people to access information at an unprecedented rate. Historically, rally organisers would need to travel to find venues. The organiser for the 1987 Summer Rally shared their experience when they had to sort out a venue for the barn dance: *"...this involved several Sundays spent cycling around the nearer parts of Wocester looking for a suitable venue"*. Imagine how time consuming that was -

68

having to physically explore the city and work out where there were venues. Today a rally can be planned through the computer, organisers can see images of venues and read reviews, which helps in the decision making process.

SSAGO has always tried to find effective and efficient ways of communicating, especially as the organisation grew in size. By 1999 SSAGO had fully embraced the internet. The Publicity Officer's job focused on updating and maintaining the website, whilst also producing *SSAGO News*. SSAGO members are known to be passionate and generous. Rather than outsourcing and paying for designers, all of the magazines mentioned throughout this book were designed by members, for members. A lot of time and dedication has been put into documenting SSAGO's history and these original sources give us unguarded insight into opinions and stories of the time. In 2013 *SSAGO News* was moved away from a publication format and into an online article format. Whilst the format has changed there is still the desire to record stories for the future. The effort put in by members has paid off because these sources allow us to understand what it was like to be a SSAGO member in the past.

Below: Extract about electronic mail from SSAGO Journal 1989 Autumn edition

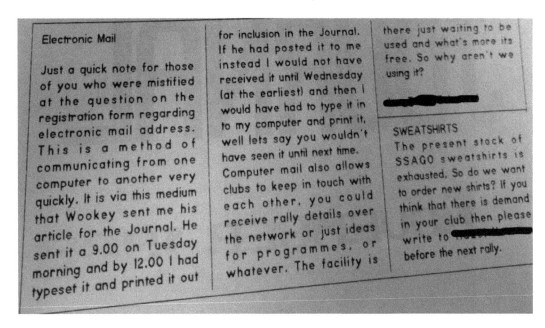

SSAGO and it's predecessor organisations magazines
1959 - 2000

Student Scout and Guide magazine
Summer 1959

Kudu magazine Issue 27 Autumn 1960

SAGO Journal 1988

SSAGO News Autumn 2000

SSAGO websites 1999 - 2022

SSAGO website 1999

SSAGO Website 2010

SSAGO Website 2019

SSAGO Website 2022

Cardiff meet Finnish Scouts, SSAGO News summer 2000 By Alison Carpenter

Extract from Cardiff Student Scout and Guide club meeting Finnish Scouts, who had found Cardiff online:

"Cardiff Student Scout and Guide society were really pleased to find that their web page had reached a similar University Group in Finland. Last Easter term Cardiff SSAGS received an email from members of the Helsinki Institute of Technology Scout and Guide group. The email explained that they were planning a Cycling trip through Wales starting in Cardiff on the 27th May.

After many emails, we arranged to meet the group. Being a Rugby day, this proved more difficult than expected and unfortunately the group had not managed to arrange accommodation for the night. We quickly managed to find a campsite, as all the youth hostels were full. Tents were put up in the rain, not unusual for Wales, we explained to the Finns! We then set about welcoming the group of 7 students with a meal in a traditional Welsh pub. Over food and drinks we began to learn about the students and their lives in Finland. A cheerful evening was spent in the pub and as we left we promised to meet them again the next day.

A trip to Cardiff Castle and the museum were enjoyed by both societies. it was then on to another pub for yet more food. Over the meal the Finnish group planned their route out of Cardiff, through the Brecon Beacons onwards... Many of Cardiff SSAGS felt tired just at the thought of the long trip that lay ahead for the Finns.

What was meant to be just one afternoon with the Finnish Scouts had turned into an extremely enjoyable weekend, presents were exchanged, many photos taken and email addresses swapped.

On Sunday evening we wished the group well for their journey, with the promise that the rain would not continue forever! Two weeks later we heard that the group had made it safely to Manchester airport and were about to board their plane home. Hopefully Cardiff SSAGS will visit Finland in the future, for now though we all need practicing on our bikes!"

Above: Independent members camp summer 2021. Created in 1981 it was a type of membership for students without a local club or who couldn't join their local club but still wanted to join the organisation for national events.

Above: SSAGO Exec members enjoying their pink onesies, Cambridge Duck Rally 2018 The internet gave SSAGO the opportunity to explore suppliers for merchandise regardless of where the supplier was located.

Chapter 8
Putting the O in SSAGO

Running SSAGO required commitment, passion and organisation. Order and direction was needed as part of the National Executive committee.

Until the 1990s SSAGO would informally ask clubs to come forward and run the upcoming rallies. There was no timeframe for this, meaning rallies might have been scheduled for many years in advance. However at the 1994 AGM it was agreed that rally bids should be made at the spring Reps and then brought to the AGM to be voted on. The new approach stopped clubs booking years ahead in the calendar and SSAGO would now only vote 4, 5 and 6 terms ahead of the current schedule. Eventually SSAGO smoothed this process out further by only bidding for events occurring in the next calendar year - which is still practiced today. Additionally bidding for rally helps clubs to understand what kind of event they would like to run. Clubs are limited to the type of local campsites near them which would be suitable for different rallies. Each rally is unique in what it needs to deliver: the Autumn Rally is the first event of the year so it needs to cater for Freshers and the cold weather, the Spring Rally needs enough space for a few hundred people at the AGM and the Summer Rally enjoys the warmer weather but tends to be smaller in size (due to people going on holiday or on other Scout and Guide trips). Not every campsite is big enough for an AGM, or the site may be particularly difficult to clean after a muddy weekend in November.

With Rally bids being decided by ballot, inevitably bids that appeal to their target market are typically the most successful. Generally cash strapped students place the location of the potential rally high on their criteria when deciding on which to vote for, as often getting to rally can cost more than the rally itself. Clubs therefore have encouraged neighbouring clubs to vote for them, as an act of friendship and because the journey time should be shorter. Thus there has always been a struggle to balance the rallies across the country; one year the rallies may all be in the north, the next they'll be in the south. This is often caused by clubs from one area deciding that the best way to have a rally close to them is to run it themselves, and thus they bid at the next AGM. Clubs with good transport links are often keen to mention their local area's 'strategic road network' at the AGM, something that has since become a running joke at most AGMs from the late 2010s onwards. The other way to entice voters is proposing a Rally with an interesting theme. Themed rallies have changed over the years as SSAGO moved away from national gatherings to discuss topics and more towards adventure and socialising. Rallies come with a theme such as periods of history (Roman, 1989; Medieval, 2010; 90s, 2017), children's parties (Inflatable, 2011; Pirates, 2013;

Superheros, 2015) or pop culture (James Bond, 2004; Blackadder, 2006; Disney, 2008), which influence the activities, food and branding of the event. Some themes have been repeated over the years, such as Birmingham's Chocolate Rally (2006 and 2019) or Bath's Roman Rally (1989, 1995 and 2020).

A new type of membership, Associate membership, was introduced towards the late 1990s and early 2000s and was implemented largely for insurance reasons. Associate members are insured, but do not gain the full membership status which includes the ability to vote. Associates are those who are no longer a student but who still provide value to either their club or the wider organisation. For example, the member may be a minibus driver or part of an upcoming rally committee. Some Associate members stay for an extra year to assist with staffing at rallies and pass their knowledge on to the next generation of SSAGO members. In the decades preceding the introduction of Associate membership, it became clear that these members held valuable information and knowledge based on their personal experiences. SSAGO's traditions and development have been maintained through word of mouth and Associates have been vessels of those traditions. One example would be the process of nominating members for funny awards at rallies, such as the Spoon of Incompetence or the Brownie Award. Starting with the 2001 'Old Gits' Rally but becoming more frequent in recent years, Associate members from multiple clubs have banded together to run rallies as opposed to a sole club. The 2017 Witan in a Weekend Rally was run by a committee who were all SSAGO Associates nicknamed 'Old Goats'. Associate rallies have typically been very successful, as associates can use their experience to plan the event without worrying about other student matters. Over time many Associates would move away from SSAGO and join SAGGA as a way to stay in touch with friends and be involved in community activities.

At the 1997 spring Reps, SSAGO launched 'regions', with the aim to improve communication between clubs and keep them in closer contact with the National Executive committee. It was challenging for the national Secretary to chase clubs for membership fees and to figure out if a club had closed or a new club had started. Having a regional representative would smooth out this process as they could then go on to inform the National Executive committee of any changes. The results of SSAGO regions were mixed.

Some regions worked well without guidance or input from the National Executive committee - they naturally came together and worked on camps or local socials. The most apparent outcome was the introduction of regional Freshers' camps, which softly introduced new members before the larger autumn rally. For some clubs it was obvious as to what region they should be in, but others have gone through phases of being determined to fit into one region then changing their mind the next year. For example during the period of 2016 - 2018 Aberystwyth was keen to create an all Wales region but Bangor wanted to be part of the Midlands region, citing difficulties with pan-Wales public transport. Meanwhile, it made sense for the south Wales clubs to join the south-west region, leaving Aberystwyth without a region at all.

Ultimately the idea never fulfilled its potential; the topic is often brought up at Reps throughout the 2010s and 2020s. Manifestos for the National Executive roles in the early 2000s and again from 2016 cite the introduction and development of regions. The most common issue is where to draw the dividing lines. Interestingly there wasn't an original East of England region, rather a south-east including London and north-west including the Midlands, so it was confusing for clubs like Cambridge who didn't know which region they belonged in. Additionally, although dividing the country was, and still is useful and logical, it has been controversial on how it should be governed. Club rivalry has also influenced how regions are divided up. For example the south-west region has sometimes offered spaces for the south west freshers camp to clubs closer to the south-east such as Reading.

In 2004 SSAGO introduced a new national event, the SSAGO Ball. Members wanted an opportunity to dress up in something smarter than their usual camping drab and have a formal sit-down event. Ball is where members can come together at the end of the academic year (around April time), to relax and celebrate. Since then the event has been hosted across the country, usually at a hotel but sometimes at more interesting locations such as Southampton's 2014 Ball on a Boat. Members enjoy spending time with their friends in a relaxed and sociable environment and it's always a fun opportunity when you can dress up. Ball has sometimes been expanded to include a weekend of activities, especially for the Friday evening and Saturday daytime. From tourist attractions to social gatherings and short hikes, it gives members the opportunity to make the most of the weekend. It is also a convenient time for the National Executive committee to go through their handover meeting with the incoming National Executive committee, concluding the year and setting up the summer tasks and objectives.

2007 was a big year for The Scouts, Girlguiding and SSAGO. The Scouts celebrated their centenary, marking 100 years since the original Brownsea Island camp and creation of the movement by Lord Baden-Powell. Just 2 years later Girlguiding had their own centenary, celebrating the beginnings of Girlguiding at Crystal Palace. For SSAGO, 2007 was the 40th anniversary of Intervarsity and Intercollegiate coming together to form an amalgamated organisation. To celebrate the occasion the Summer Rally that year became a reunion camp at Sudbrooke Park, Lincolnshire on the theme *Summer of Love*. Being the first birthday event for SSAGO the committee had to design the programme from scratch, although it was largely based on a standard rally format. The organising committee planned the event through Microsoft Messenger and face to face meetings at the rallies leading up to the event. There was a campfire and firework show on Friday night and on Saturday they had silly games in the morning and offsite activities in Lincoln in the afternoon. On Sunday they had on site carnival games such as a bouncy castle and the Chief Guide visited and spoke to everyone. Most people who attended were current or recently graduated members of SSAGO and there were some SAGGA members too.

Over the 2000 - 2010 period, SSAGO changed the way it governed itself and members found creative ways to streamline processes and utilise technology. SSAGO was able to improve on the diverse events it would run including a range of themes and the new formal ball. Freshers events were a regular occurrence in the calendar and it was the passion of the membership that drove SSAGO into the best organisation it could be. There were always people who wanted to run for the National Executive committee, bringing their own ambitions and aiming to improve their predecessor's work.

Above: Members chatting over a drink at Womball 2021.

Above: Lancaster members dancing at Spring Rally 2020.

Above: Southampton members enjoying camping at Duck rally summer 2017.

Above: Members supporting Wintercamp 2019.

Cutlery Cup Award

2007 was also the year the first national award was introduced, the *Cutlery Cup*. Introduced by Will Carr (Manchester) and Jenny Mcdougall (St Andrews). It was created to celebrate a member's achievement whether in SSAGO, The Scouts or Girlguiding in the community. As part of the award members are issued Honorary membership, this is a form of lifetime membership without voting rights.

Below left: Jude Balmire winner of the Cutlery Cup 2022.
Below right: Cutlery Cup Award.

Mascots

Mascots are toy animals that represent and belong to SSAGO clubs. It's not clear why mascots were acquired, possibly inspired from the American varsity sporting groups. One of the oldest known club mascots is Oxford's Eric the Panda who joined the club in 1974. Birmingham's mascot is called Scarface, who was bought in the 1970s. Over the decades their face has worn down and it has been replaced. The process involved taking off the old face then creating and stitching a new one. The old "faces" are kept in Birmingham University's library alongside the club archives.

Around the 1980s through to 1990s the Bristol University club had a mascot named Herbert. The bear was looked after for a couple of decades. The club closed in the late 1990s then revived around 2015. When the members tracked down the owner they had just thrown it out two weeks prior to receiving the club's email!

Members will attempt to steal mascots during rallies, whether that's because someone left it unattended or maybe by the slip of the hand. At the end of the camp clubs have to do a forfeit to get their mascot back, often silly games such as wheel burrows in the mud or a water fight. When club mascots become too old to be stolen they are retired and a new mascot brought in. Some particularly old or delicate mascots are labelled non-stealable. If a non-stealable mascot is stolen a forfeit is given to the club that stole it, so it is important to know which mascots can or can't be stolen.

Mascot stealing is a contentious topic with people questioning the legitimacy of stealing out of people's hands and to what extent force can be used. A policy document was written to iron out the rules from what counts as a mascot, when it can be stolen. Some might argue too much time is spent on discussing trivial matters, others believe it is a highly important aspect of SSAGO's identity.

During the late 2010s the Manchester University club appointed a Fresher to be their club mascot. Usually a different person at each rally and a slightly harder object to 'steal'. Members would attempt to pick them up and carry them to a member of the National Executive committee.

Above: Mascots at the mascot table Ball 2022.

Above: Member holding a variety of mascots.

Above: National SSAGO Executive committee 2020-2021 and their mascots.

Above: Birmingham's mascots at Womball 2021.

Chapter 9
Getting back to business

Students wanted to improve the way the organisation was operating. From formalising processes and policies to solidifying itself as a charity. These things would upgrade SSAGO into the 21st century.

From 2007 onwards both the organisation and individuals expanded onto social media and it changed the way we behaved and communicated within society. Whilst young people used it to connect with friends, it was also used by the National Executive committee to share information, advertise relevant events and bring the community together. For example, groups were made on social media for participants of the next rally and through the instant notifications feature rally organisers were able to send out information fast. If there was a sudden change in plan, event organisers could post updates online for participants to see it within seconds. Social media also furthered SSAGO's capacity for self-promotion beyond in-person events.

In 2016 the Publicity Officer along with members of SSAGO produced a video advertising SSAGO. The video featured footage from the recent Summer Rally as well as clips from club meetings and other national events. It was published around A-Level results day in August - an important day when many young people find out which university they will be heading to. The video was a great format to present to prospective members what SSAGO is all about.

Website improvements and features also contributed to SSAGO's development and expansion during the late 2010s. In 2015 a new website launched with improved modifications including an events system, joining page for new members, a club map and directory. It also expanded the resources section for documentation including policy documents, meeting minutes and factsheets. The website had a fresh design for better admin abilities and user experience. Since 2015 the website has continued to be updated and improved based on member feedback. For example, online voting was introduced in 2016 allowing all members to vote in the AGM, including those who couldn't attend the Spring Rally. SSAGO's archiving capacity has advanced also; the archives have helped to date back past events and SSAGO now logs awards online including previous winners. There is a mascot page to find out about what they are, what club they belonged to and most importantly which you can steal at the next national event. The website modifications were implemented by students for students and the features have helped to share knowledge, promote events and stay relevant in a technological world.

88

In 2016 the Publicity Officer introduced a rally newsletter: an engaging, amusing and all encompassing publication for members to read whilst on rally. It was written every evening at camp for a morning release. Using the website, members could submit stories and pictures about their time at the rally. The newsletter at the 2016 Summer Rally was a great success so it was continued into the autumn and became a tradition for the following years. It was a new avenue for members to engage with publicity by providing their use of language, interest in design or writing and editing stories. Of course this is not the first newsletter the organisation produced and the rally newsletter will become an important part of the archive in the future.

During the early 2010s SSAGO started to consider whether it should become a charity. It is still an ongoing discussion. The road to charity status would be difficult and take many years however many believed the benefits outweighed the costs. It became an organisational goal, thus the National Executive committee researched into becoming a Charity Incorporated Organisation (CIO). The charity status would give SSAGO an improved reputation, helping its outlook and visibility and a range of financial benefits. However, with benefits also comes acceptable disadvantages such as the need for greater financial scrutiny and to overhaul the constitution, which would be a big task. It is interesting to note that the discussions during this period mirrored those of the formation of SSAGO fifty years prior. The benefits of being a CIO would not be felt by the membership, however it would impact the National Executive committee in what was believed to be a largely positive way. Similarly, the formation of a unified organisation in 1967 was to benefit the running of SSAGO, rather than the individual member experience. Understandably it was difficult to convince the membership that the process was worth it when it wouldn't impact them directly.

Throughout 2017 a Memorandum of Agreement was being drafted as a relationship agreement between SSAGO, The Scouts and Girlguiding. It set out how the organisations would work together and support each other to promote the development of Scouting and Guiding. The document covered areas including insurance, accident and incident reporting and communication. In the years following the draft, the National Executive committee struggled to maintain a consistent relationship with Girlguiding. Every year there was a new designated staff member to take the role as SSAGO's link. SSAGO had to re-introduce itself to Girlguiding every time thus it became difficult to get the document reviewed and signed off. The process was tedious and difficult for SSAGO; SSAGO relies on its parent organisations but they aren't always there for them, an unfortunate situation, but one that doesn't prevent the membership from making the most of what it can do.

As a running tradition during the 2000s the National Executive Committee would wear brightly coloured hoodies to make themselves clearly known to the membership at busy national events. A National Executive committee couldn't own the same colour as a previous committee until all members had moved on. By 2017 the choice was limited and so the chair decided to form a clear brand for the organising committee of SSAGO. This was called Team Pink and included the assistants that supported the National Executive committee. All of the branding such as hoodies and t-shirts were bright pink and florescent yellow, making them identifiable at rallies. Before 2017 there had only been two or three assistants, the Webmaster, Notifications Officer and Quartermaster. But in 2017 three more assistants were appointed: the Archivist, International Officer and SAGGA Representative. Team Pink was now formed of five elected National Executive officers and six appointed assistants, the biggest team in the history of the organisation. It was necessary to appoint these roles to delegate specific responsibilities, however each assistant was given a line manager who was closely related to their role. For example the Treasurer was the line manager for the Quartermaster, as the latter's role frequently required access to the SSAGO bank accounts. Tasks and responsibilities for the National Executive committee grew over the 2010s with the scope of the role resembling a level of commitment comparable to a full time job.

It was therefore necessary to get skilled and knowledgeable people onboard to help behind the scenes. For example, whilst the 2016 Witan to Berlin didn't include any international student Scouts and Guides, it did promote the membership's interest in rebuilding its international links. The International Officer was the perfect person to work on relations with other student Scout and Guide clubs, as close as Ireland and as far as Australia. SSAGO is unique in its format and running, thus has been frequently contacted for advice on how other student Scout and Guide clubs can run a similar organisation in their home country.

SSAGO's direction during the 2010s was largely influenced by the introduction of social media. It changed the way we communicated and therefore developed SSAGO's ability to promote itself and form an online community of current and past members. SSAGO's National Executive committees focused on pressing matters such as becoming a CIO, though that story doesn't have an ending. It is interesting to see the membership trying to develop the organisation to something more than what it currently is. There was a growing understanding that the National Executive committee members needed Assistants. By expanding Team Pink roles SSAGO was able to work on more projects. Tasks were delegated to the Assistants who didn't have the same pressures as the National Executive committee. Assistants were appointed and can stay in their role of an unspecified amount of time. SSAGO built on its traditions, brought new ones in and learnt from mistakes made to improve the way it functioned.

Below left: First rally newsletter, Bedrock Bugle. Summer Rally 2016.
Below right: Tea Times, Spring Rally 2017.

Above: Members at the annual general meeting Spring Rally 2020.

Above: Members enjoying spring Rally 2020.

Above: Members at SSAGO's 50th Anniversary camp 2017, amused at how the location of Aberystwyth isn't accurate on SSAGO pull up banners.

Above: Incoming and outgoing Chairpersons at Ball 2022.

Full membership survey

In 2017 SSAGO launched what was believed to be its first full membership survey in a bid to further understand what members thought of the organisation. Questions were asked on a variety of topics including national events, the relationship with The Scouts and Girlguiding and where SSAGO could improve.

When asked what was the most enjoyable element of SSAGO, members responded that they liked communicating and working coherently with other individuals. National events were a particular highlight as it gives members the opportunity to be a participant rather than a leader as well as the opportunity to let off some steam and get away from university life. Being surrounded by those with similar interests was also noted as, regardless of where they come from in the country, all student Scouts and Guides are welcome in SSAGO.

"I love being part of SSAGO as it is a great big community where you get to make lots of new friends and have great new experiences! I have really enjoyed my time in SSAGO and I want to see others getting the same benefit out of it as I did!"

When asked about how National Events could be improved one comment noted that national events *"...don't seem to focus much around the values of Scouting/Guiding. Perhaps we could focus more on the leadership roles SSAGO members have in their districts, and encourage people to share ideas on how to run sessions with their groups so that when SSAGO members go home, they can bring back new ideas to help improve scouting back home."* As mentioned previously, rallies used to be an opportunity to discuss topics relating to Students, Scouts and Guides but moved away from this to have a recreational feel. It is interesting to see that in 2017 there were some members who still wanted SSAGO to be a place of discussion.

Members were asked about how SSAGO could improve its relations with The Scouts and Girlguiding. There were a lot of comments about the lack of awareness of SSAGO prior to going to university. Members felt strongly that Scout groups and Guide units should be informed about SSAGO and leaders should inform their members as they reach their final year in the section. When SSAGO is mentioned the emphasis should be that young people can continue in The Scouts and Girlguiding by giving back to the community. The main pull factor for members is to continue the passion they have yet unfortunately not everyone is made aware of how to achieve this.

Following the success of the 2017 survey another survey was conducted in 2020. It largely had the same questions, with a few extra questions included to suit what was now a slightly different generation of students. One of the new questions was centred around inclusion and diversity. Members commented about the lack of members from non-white backgrounds, which is also seen in The Scouts and Girlguiding movements. The membership wanted to see the introduction of an inclusion officer. The role would be focused on ensuring that measures would be considered for members with disabilities. For example, wheelchair accessible campsites and personalising rally programmes for their specific needs. The officer would also sit on Team Pink and would be a link between the voices of the members and the running of SSAGO.

There were echoed comments about the relationship with The Scouts and Girlguiding. Members still hadn't seen improvements from The Scouts and Girlguiding on promoting SSAGO. The members mentioned that on a local and regional basis leaders were not always aware of SSAGO, or they had heard of SSAGO but didn't fully appreciate what it could offer. The survey also highlighted that there is a correlation between where Scout and Guide groups are not within reach of a university then they are unlikely to have heard of SSAGO. Therefore, those young people are more likely to leave the movements as they turn eighteen and move on. Many members are keen to see SSAGO as a natural progress from Rangers/Explorers for students starting at university. However, this has been difficult to achieve without total support from the parent movements.

A member's comment about Scouting experience in their local community. *"People in both organisations are more aware of what SSAGO is and not just using them as extra volunteers because they think students have loads of time to volunteer. When communicating with Scouts in the local area, to say we have freshers that are interested in helping, they don't reply. Then when they need helpers for camps or events, they expect us to be able to help,*

95

whilst giving us very little notice. For example: a local Scout leader will post on the society's Facebook group that they need helpers at a camp in 5 days time but then when we post saying we have x amount of freshers that want to volunteer, they aren't interested." Gathering comments such as these can help the National Executive committee focus their efforts. It's not just about letting people know about SSAGO but furthering that knowledge into how Scouting and Guiding at a local level can work closely with the SSAGO club.

Below: Member signing the ball book at Once Upon a Ball Spring 2022. A record of who attended the event and their message.

Above: Members asking questions at annual general meting Spring Rally 2020.

Above: Members listening to the outgoing chair at the annual general meting Spring Rally 2020.

SSAGO Scout Active Support Unit (SASU)

Wider support and commitment towards the Scout and Guide movements has always been at the heart of SSAGO's aims and values. In June 1948 the Baden Powell Guild of Old Scouts was formed as a separate association for older Scouts, it had its own training programme and provided active support to the local districts. In the 1970's it was reviewed and the Old Scouts association was replaced with a district focused group called Scout Fellowship. The Fellowship scheme grew in numbers over the following decades however by the early 2000s another review was conducted. The results led to another name change in 2009 to what we know today as Scout Active Support. It was a flexible way people could be part of The Scouts, including assisting at camps, Jamborees and informally for their district. By 2017 Scout Active Support Units (SASU) were firmly established all over the country and included pre-existing groups such as SAGGA and the Queen Scout Working Party.

The build up to SSAGO forming a SASU started in 2001 when the National Executive committee attended Gilwell Reunion and found it to be a new venture for publicising SSAGO to both leaders and other students. More events were added to the calendar such as Gilwell 24, Wellies and Wristbands, Wintercamp and local jamborees. SSAGO would usually run a backwards cooking base or similar activity where Scouts and Guides could informally chat to SSAGO members whilst warming up at the campfire. Over time SSAGO's presence at The Scouts' and Girlguiding's events became formalised and came to be known as *SSAGO Support*. Prior to this SSAGO did not have a regular event where it could promote itself and relied on word of mouth and Freshers fayre stalls. SSAGO Support was a mutually beneficial arrangement. Events involved SSAGO members by staffing activities and it was an opportunity for young people, especially those aged 17 or 18, to meet SSAGO members before they headed off to university.

During the mid 2010s, as a method to improve the Disclosure and Barring Service (DBS) check process, SSAGO set out to form a SASU branch of the organisation. Members attending as support staff at events could be placed on the SASU list on the system, allowing The Scouts to conduct a DBS check for any members who do not already hold a Scouting or Guiding role. The SASU branch of SSAGO allowed members to give back to Scouting and Guiding where they might not be able to do so with their commitment to studies and their clubs. Although not an obvious or exciting development, becoming a SASU was a big step in SSAGO's history as it strengthened its relationships with The Scouts and Girlguiding during this period.

Above: Members enjoying backwards cooking Wintercamp 2019.

Above: Members supporting Wintercamp 2020 by running a challenge competition. Participants were tasked with 10 challenges, and if they completed all of them they got a badge

50th Anniversary milestone

SSAGO turned 50 years old in 2017, marking half a century since the amalgamation of Intervarsity and Intercollegiate. It was important that a special event was held to mark the occasion, thus a reunion camp was held at Scout Park, London in September 2017 with all past members invited. Whilst the students who organised it did have experience running clubs, being on the National Executive committee and holding Scouting/Guiding roles, it was still a challenging weekend to organise. Planning an event of this magnitude required a lot of hard work and patience. SAGGA played a big role in supporting the camp committee during the lead up and at the weekend by providing advice and programme ideas - such as a cheese and wine stall. The camp was a success with 300 people present for the birthday celebrations. There were a range of activities on site such as crafts, badge swapping and Quidditch. People could also go off-site and see all that London had to offer with its museums and tourist attractions. As expected for a SSAGO event there was a Cedeilh dance on the Saturday evening and home baked birthday cake for all to enjoy. The weekend was an opportunity to meet older members who were part of clubs from different generations. The common interest helped people to bond together, and with club's largely maintaining their necker colours over the years, it wasn't difficult to identify who was from which club.

Below: Anniversary challenge badge. Each section had specific requirements to be awarded the badge.

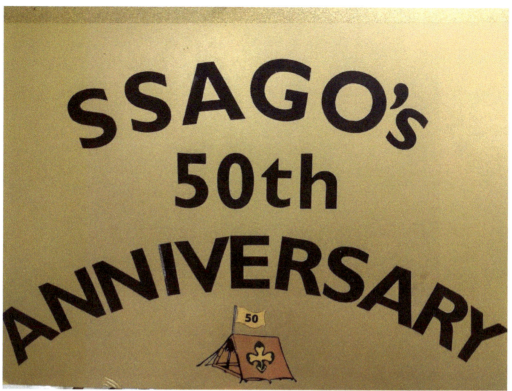
Above: SSAGO Anniversary card front cover.

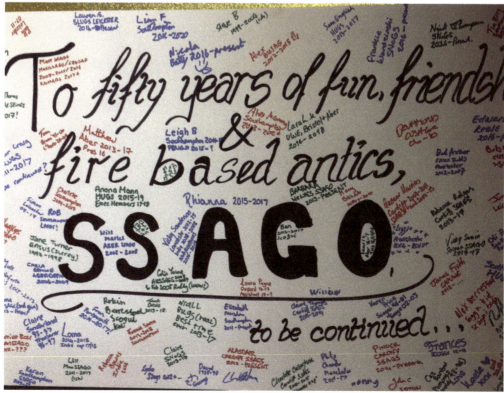
Above: SSAGO Anniversary card inside with attendee's names and belonging clubs.

Above: Group photo at the 50th Anniversary camp 2017.

Above: Members at popup museum 50th Anniversary camp 2017.

Above: Members dancing at Ceilidh, 50 Anniversary camp 2017.

Above: SAGGA members at 50th Anniversary 2017.

Chapter 10
Looking up in lockdown

In 2020 SSAGO was looking forward to another exciting year. Nobody expected the Spring Rally to be the last in-person event SSAGO would see for 17 months.

When news of the COVID-19 virus started to spread at the start of 2020 no one could predict what its lasting impact would be across the world. Within weeks of the Spring Rally, news of the pandemic had reached the UK public. Many people thought it would be short-lived, SSAGO would go through an odd period and then things would go back to normal. However, in line with the UK Government's announcement of a nationwide lockdown in mid March, all social activities stopped and learning went online. Witan was postponed for 12 months, the bookings moved to summer 2021. National event committees were asked if they wanted to postpone their event or cancel it. There was a general feeling that the spread of the virus would be short term and life would largely return to normal by the autumn of 2020.

For the elected National Executive committee who were starting their term in April 2020, the pandemic was an unprecedented experience. The outgoing National Executive committee and the incoming National Executive committee had to re-organise their handover into multiple online meetings. Unfortunately their first task together boiled down to holding SSAGO together whilst cancelling events in an ever evolving situation. For many event committees their planning had matured and their events were nearly ready to accept bookings and looked forward to welcoming SSAGO. Ultimately none of the 2020 National events were delivered in their typical format, which was a huge disappointment for everyone. Whilst there was some lifting of restrictions over the summer that allowed small groups to meet, all national events in 2020 were cancelled. It was an overwhelming experience for the incoming National Executive committee to cancel the calendar whilst working out their individual roles. However, they were able to use their Scouting and Guiding experiences as leaders to put in the time SSAGO needed from them. It was not the best start to a National Executive year, but the membership understood the decisions that were made and supported the organising committees.

"It was a time we realised what we were in for." - Amy Fanklin, Members officer 2020-2021

An online chat room called Discord was set up the same week the country was put into lockdown. On the Discord server, topic specific chat rooms are called channels and these were created for conversations on gardening, arts and craft, archives, photos, gaming, fitness and much more. A team came together to create a weekly programme of online badges for SSAGO members to earn. Some badges were original such as crafting, fitness and exploring the archives and others were from the Scouting or Guiding programmes across all sections. The "badges at home" were a way for members to engage with one another despite the lockdown being in-place. To earn the badges, members could meet up virtually to work on the requirements or do an activity on their own and then share what they made or did on the Discord channel. The server allowed members to connect with their clubs and other people across the UK who shared common interests. Typically clubs would meet in person and then would only mix with other clubs at national or regional events. However, through Discord and virtual meetings members could meet anyone across the UK and overseas at any time. What was once a weekly social with club members became weekly socials for all SSAGO members. The server was used throughout the lockdowns during 2020 and 2021 and the universal access to every member allowed the organisation to blur the lines between clubs.

The national lockdown meant most people were unable to spend Easter 2020 seeing family and socialising as they normally would. SSAGO put together an online Easter Egg hunt where various virtual eggs were hidden across the SSAGO website, SSAGO Minecraft server and Discord server. Clues were used to help members find the eggs and explore the website - from news articles to old event photo galleries. The game was fun for all ages, with SSAGO inviting SAGGA and their families to take part. Elsewhere members from clubs across the UK set up a podcast team with the help of the National Executive committee. Using Discord features such as chat and voice chat they were able to meet regularly to plan and record their own SSAGO podcast. The podcast channel was open to everyone in the server thus anyone could bring their skills forward, whether as an editor or presenter. Outside this there were regular and spontaneous online gaming sessions, Dungeons and Dragon campaigns, book swaps, baking competitions, secret santas and much more.

Because the City of Steel Ball was cancelled the introduction of a new SSAGO Award was pushed to an online awards event in August 2020. The award was introduced by the publicity officer, Reuben Cone. The award was to recognise a committee for their hard work at a national event or at club level in a similar vein to the Cutlery Cup. A colander was chosen because it would match the culinary theme of it's sister award and because being on a committee could be quite draining! The very first Committee Colander was given to the Birmingham club committee 2019-2020, for their efforts in running a successful birthday camp, Rally and growing the club all in one year. The award was a good addition to the range of awards possible for a SSAGO member to be nominated for.

Despite most people's expectations, by autumn of 2020 the pandemic was still ongoing and the UK had been through several lockdowns. The summer is typically a quiet time in the SSAGO calendar; students go home and the National Executive committee can focus on their personal objectives they have for their roles. However, for the then National Executive committee it was a time of grieving. For what was meant to be an exciting and adventurous year had become a difficult journey to keep SSAGO afloat and ride through the pandemic storm. It was a time for them to consider how as an individual they can make the most of the circumstances and make their role relevant amongst the chaos.

As the autumn period rolled in students initially went back to University campuses, with the aim to go ahead with face to face teaching. However the Government changed tact, moving education online to derail rising COVID-19 cases. This left some students stranded on campus for a period of time, mostly spending their time on Discord and e-learning. For the National Executive committee their primary focus was to package COVID-19 guidance into clear documentation. It wasn't easy to balance guidance from The Scouts, Girlguiding, Student Unions and the Government. In some cases guidance conflicted! Do you follow The Scouts or your Students Union? There was never a right answer.

The autumn rally hosted by Southampton became the first online Rally when they turned their programme into a virtual event. Participants were sent a box of items for the weekend including handmade bunting, Lego, mini marshmallows and other items to create an at home camping experience. It was a fun weekend for members to do something different and break up what was becoming a monotonous lifestyle at home.

108

As time moved on and it became apparent that the 2020-2021 year would end how it started, plans had to be made for the upcoming AGM in February. The National Executive committee couldn't copy from past experiences, the disruptive nature of the pandemic meant they had to be bold and act with the knowledge and guidance they had. They all did an excellent job to stick together for the whole year and help SSAGO through it. For the first time ever, Reps and the AGM were held online. They used the online voting function allowing them to run the AGM as close to normal as possible and held the husting through video call. The National Executive committee had to ignore some of the constitutional requirements of the AGM, notably the full calendar year of events was not voted on. This would give the incoming National Executive committee flexibility when planning the 2021-2022 calendar over the 2021 summer. It was an odd time for the outgoing National Executive committee who were now echoing their handover experience again with their successors through online meetings and virtual events.

The first in-person national event to return was in September 2021: Birmingham's WomBall at Rough Close campsite. The festival style event was an alternative take from the traditional formal ball. Knowing that an outdoor event would be safer and could carry a higher capacity, the club changed their event in response to the pandemic. The event saw nearly 100 members come together and meet in person for the first time since February 2020. The event was a relaxing introduction to the upcoming academic year which saw members feeling enthused for future in person events and getting back to camping. It was also an opportunity to meet friends they had met through Discord face to face for the first time.

The pandemic was the single most disruptive event in SSAGO's history. For the first time ever, SSAGO was unable to function under its usual circumstances, clubs couldn't hold face to face meetings and members couldn't go to national events. Like many other organisations SSAGO embraced the technological world and this helped them to stay connected with each other. SSAGO's membership retention relies on successful events where members can build friendships and have adventures so moving this online wasn't easy. Despite the setbacks caused by the pandemic, SSAGO adapted to the world around it, as it has always managed to do. What will come of the lasting effect of the pandemic? Only time will tell and perhaps it will be another decade till we can truly understand the impact. Nothing could replicate a face to face meeting or the buzz of a national event, but SSAGO's efforts were good enough for the interim, knowing that normality would one day return.

As SSAGO currently experiences the fallout of one of the most pivotal moments in its history, this book ends on an interesting note. We've already seen some signs of post pandemic recovery but it is likely SSAGO has a lot of work to do in the years ahead. It needs to refind its feet and establish its goals for the rest of the decade. Will SSAGO continue the traditions its predecessors worked hard to implement? Or perhaps it will form new traditions in an online world driven by thinking outside of the box. Only in time will we know the answers to these, and many more, questions.

Below: Committee colander.

Above: Birmingham Scout and Guide Club Committee Colander winners for 2021. For an outstanding year jammed packed with big events such as their 90th Anniversary Camp.

Above: Liverpool Science Jamboree Committee Colander winners for 2022. They prepared boxes of science experiments for over 1200 Beavers, Rainbows, Cubs and Brownies.

Above: Members at spring rally 2020.

Above: Two members of the 2020/2021 National Executive committee finally at a face to face event. Womball 2021

Above: Members having fun during the silent disco at spring rally 2020.

Above: Ceilidh dancing at spring Rally 2020.

Epilogue

It's been over hundred years since the first Rover Crews and Ranger Units began on university campuses. In that time new generations of student Scouts and Guides have founded two organisations, survived a World War, subverted societal expectations, amalgamated a new organisation, established their own traditions, integrated new technologies and have powered through a pandemic. All the while the results of their efforts, SSAGO as an organisation, has continued to remain relevant and suit the needs of the current cohort of students.

However SSAGO's success in remaining relevant is ironic considering how strikingly similar experiences are had by every member to have been a part of SSAGO. The social activities have largely remained the same; members have always camped, served their community and made friends both inside and outside of their club.

The SSAGO Rally of today is much the same as the one of yesteryear. Although Mike Day noted how Intercollegiate and Intervarsity rallies were surprisingly similar, he would be equally amazed that his comments still rang true to SSAGO rallies exactly 60 years later. If he were to stand in the corner of a rally marquee and look out across the floor, between the chaos of the ceilidh, the mascots and the heated debate of reps, only one thing can be certain: the people may change but SSAGO remains very much the same.

SSAGO's ever evolving membership but ability to continue doing what it always has done is testament to the original formula. Members of SSAGO aren't involved for long periods of time. Most members stay for the duration of their university course, but sooner or later the next batch of Freshers arrive. They give a *fresh* view of the organisation and ensure the SSAGO formula remains relevant for current members. They may not make the right decision every time, and not all guarantees are kept, but the passion from the membership continually drives it forward.

That passion to make SSAGO better can be seen throughout the organisation. From those who run weekly meetings for their peers, the National Event committees who step up to run rallies, and the National Executive Committee who keep everything together. Everyone puts in the time and effort into the roles they hold and without these people SSAGO wouldn't exist.

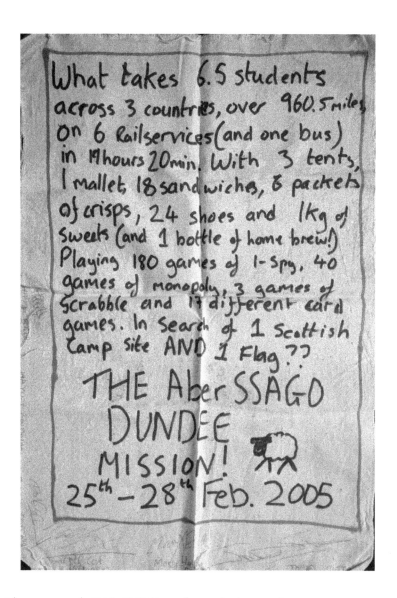

Above: The Aberystwyth SSAGO Dundee mission written on a tea towel. Aberystwyth University SSAGO Archives

Timeline of SSAGO

1920 Rover Scouts and Ranger Guides at University.

1947 First Intervarsity Rally held in Beaudesert, Stafford, organised by Birmingham. They were week long (7-10 days) as a summer camp every year until 1960.

1956 Federation of Scout and Guide Clubs formed in response to college students being declined entry into Intervarsity.
Antelope horn and 10 Gunnies donated to Intervarsity.

1957 Intercollegiate formed for colleges and training colleges.

1959 Oxford invites European countries equivalent to Intervarsity to rally. This lead to the first Witan called 'Meeting of the Wise'.
Scout and Guide Graduate Association (SAGGA) formed as a response to being too old for Intervarsity and dubbed 'Peter Pans'.

1960 Rallys move to weekend events in Spring, Summer and Autumn.

1964 Talks of a united organisation began between Intervarsity, Intercollegiate and Scout HQ. Largely due to increase in the number of higher education institutions being granted university status.

1967 National Student Scout & Guide Organisation (SSAGO) formed. At Spring Rally the official name was voted on and they agreed on the constitution.
The Scout Association runs a national survey called the Advance Party Report which led to Rover Scouts and Senior Scouts being abolished.

1970s Questions over where the organisation was heading, with changes in the structure and nature of rallies. No more were Rallies a place of intellectual discussions. One member wrote "SSAGO is not a travel agency". - Kudu Notes 1970.

1978   Publicity Secretary introduced and produces the publicity materials for SSAGO such as, SSAGO Journal and Kudu Notes.

1981   Assistant Secretary replaced with Publicity Secretary.
Independent Membership introduced for members without a club or couldn't commit the time to their local club.

1984   Witan is held in Italy where all attending countries received a ceremonial plate by the Libyan contingent. The UKs plate later got renamed "The Gadaffy 'Duck' Plate".

1987   Discussions between SAGGA, Girlguiding and The Scouts lead to the "Scouting and Education report" which changed SSAGO's registration process.

1990s   SSAGO continues to grow and modernise through the introduction of email and internet.

1996   The Scouts form the Programme Review Group to help bring Scouting into the modern age. Advance Party Report is now out of date!

1997   SSAGO goes online with it's first website.

1999   The Scouts direct contact is lost due to financial cuts with no clear replacement.

2003   SSAGO's constitution was rewritten and brought into the 21st Century.

2004   First national annual ball.

2007   Cutlery Cup/Honorary membership award created.

2012   First 'New Style' Witan to Kandersteg International Scout Campsite in Switzerland.

2013   'SSAGO News' goes online, no more printed press.

2015   Membership system and new rally website created.

2016   New website introduced with up to date resources: SSAGO map, club directory, club pages, resources and sign up page.

2017   50 years of SSAGO celebrated.

2020   COVID-19 Pandemic hits world wide, SSAGO goes online including badges at home and zoom meetings.
Committee Colander introduced.

2021   Womball in September first national event since Spring 2020.

Above: Assortment of Kudu magazines.
Below: Members at spring rally 2020.

Glossary

Affiliated club Linked to a university, affiliated clubs also register with SSAGO so that they can attend events and receive extra perks such as insurance and discount codes.

Committee Colander Awarded to recognise the hard work and dedication that committees have shown as part of SSAGO clubs or local, national or international events.

Cutlery Cup Awarded to recognise a current SSAGO member who has done great work for SSAGO as well as Scouting and Guiding.

Explorer Scouts A section of The Scouts for both girls and boys aged 14 to 18.

Girlguiding The UK's largest girl-only youth organisation.

Hesley Wood/Kudu Bird Carved Antelope horn in the shape of a bird gifted to SSAGO by Sir Harold West.

Honourable member Awarded as a type of membership by the SSAGO National Executive committee in recognition of exceptional service to SSAGO, or as a result of the role they hold. Winners of the Cutlery cup also become Honorary Members of SSAGO.

Intercollegiate SSAGO's predecessor organisation for students studying at Colleges and Polytechnics.

Intervarsity SSAGO's predecessor organisation for students studying at university.

Mascots A toy representing the SSAGO club, usually an animal that represents the university or place.

Rally A national weekend camping event usually hosted by a SSAGO club for SSAGO members.

Ranger A member of the Senior Section within Girlguiding. For example, a Ranger unit at a university.

Rover Scouts A section of The Scouts for men aged 18+. Active years 1918 - 2003

Senior Section A section of Girlguiding offering different ways to be a member such as Young Leader and Ranger.

Scout Active Support Unit (SASU) A group that provides support to delivering the youth programme of the Scouts. Active years 1916 - 1967.

Scout and Guide Graduate Association (SAGGA) An organisation for anyone who want to join but primarily aimed at graduates.

Scout Network Replacing Rover Scouts in 2003. A section of The Scouts for girls and boys aged 18 to 25.

Student Scout and Guide Organisation (SSAGO) A non-uniformed organisation that enables students to continue or begin their Scouting or Guiding journey whilst at College or University.

The Scouts Youth organisation for both boys and girls.

Venture Scouts A section of The Scouts for boys and girls aged 14 to 20. Later became Explorer Scouts.

Witan An international camp for Student Scout and Guides from across the world.

About the author

Larah Korrison has been involved with The Scouts since she was 8 years old. She went on to achieve the top awards including, the Queen Scout Award, Explorer Belt, and the Duke of Edinburgh Gold award. Having an interest in history from a young age she chose to study it at the University of the West of England. Whilst there she was involved in the student Scout and Guide club. In 2017 Larah combined her training from her master's course in Archives Administration and Scouting to become the first archivist for SSAGO. Over the next 4 years Larah visited a range of university archives including: University of Bristol, University of Southampton, and University of Cambridge. Larah brought together what she had researched and learned, to display a mini museum at the SSAGO 50th anniversary camp in 2017. Larah continued to add to the SSAGO archive collection and promote it through social media. In 2021 Larah retired from her role as archivist and she was awarded Honourable membership to SSAGO for her exceptional work as archivist. Shortly afterwards, she decided to bring her wealth of knowledge together into this book.

Printed in the USA
CPSIA information can be obtained
at www.ICGtesting.com
LVHW070415041023
760080LV00013B/160